D1560630

CRIMINAL
INVESTIGATIONS

DRUG CRIME

CRIMINAL INVESTIGATIONS

CRIMINAL
INVESTIGATIONS

DRUG CRIME

MICHAEL BENSON

CONSULTING EDITOR: **JOHN L. FRENCH**,

CRIME SCENE SUPERVISOR,
BALTIMORE POLICE CRIME LABORATORY

CHELSEA HOUSE
PUBLISHERS

An imprint of Infobase Publishing

CRIMINAL INVESTIGATIONS: Drug Crime

Chelsea House
An imprint of Infobase Publishing
132 West 31st Street
New York NY 10001

Library of Congress Cataloging-in-Publication Data
Benson, Michael.
Drug crime / Michael Benson ; John L. French, consulting editor. — 1st ed.
    p. cm. — (Criminal investigations)
Includes bibliographical references and index.
ISBN-13: 978-0-7910-9407-5 (alk. paper)
ISBN-10: 0-7910-9407-3 (alk. paper)
1. Drug abuse and crime—United States. 2. Drug traffic—United States.
3. Narcotic laws—United States. 4. Criminal investigation—
United States. I. French, John L. II. Title.
HV5825.B46 2009
364.1'770973—dc22   2008027691

Chelsea House books are available at special discounts when purchased
in bulk quantities for businesses, associations, institutions,
or sales promotions. Please call our Special Sales Department
in New York at (212) 967-8800 or (800) 322-8755.

You can find Chelsea House on the World Wide Web at
http://www.chelseahouse.com

Text design by Erika K. Arroyo
Cover design by Ben Peterson

Cover: U.S. Customs Inspectors at the Paseo Del Norte port of entry
examine the 70 pounds of marijuana found in a false gas tank
in a car in November 2001.

Printed in the United States of America

Bang EJB 10 9 8 7 6 5 4 3 2 1

This book is printed on acid-free paper.

All links and Web addresses were checked and verified to be
correct at the time of publication. Because of the dynamic nature
of the Web, some addresses and links may have changed
since publication and may no longer be valid.

Contents

Foreword

In 2000 there were 15,000 murders in the United States. During that same year about a half million people were assaulted, 1.1 million cars were stolen, 400,000 robberies took place, and more than 2 million homes and businesses were broken into. All told, in the last year of the twentieth century, there were more than 11 million crimes committed in this country.*

In 2000 the population of the United States was approximately 280 million people. If each of the above crimes happened to a separate person, only 4 percent of the country would have been directly affected. Yet everyone is in some way affected by crime. Taxes pay patrolmen, detectives, and scientists to investigate it, lawyers and judges to prosecute it, and correctional officers to watch over those convicted of committing it. Crimes against businesses cause prices to rise as their owners pass on the cost of theft and security measures installed to prevent future losses. Tourism in cities, and the money it brings in, may rise and fall in part due to stories about crime in their streets. And every time someone is shot, stabbed, beaten, or assaulted, or when someone is jailed for having committed such a crime, not only they suffer but so may their friends, family, and loved ones. Crime affects everyone.

It is the job of the police to investigate crime with the purpose of putting the bad guys in jail and keeping them there, hoping thereby to punish past crimes and discourage new ones. To accomplish this a police officer has to be many things: dedicated, brave, smart, honest, and imaginative. Luck helps, but it's not required. And there's one more virtue that should be associated with law enforcement. A good police officer is patient.

Patience is a virtue in crime fighting because police officers and detectives know something that most criminals don't. It's not a secret, but most lawbreakers don't learn it until it is too late. Criminals who make money robbing people, breaking into houses, or stealing cars; who live by dealing drugs or committing murder; who spend their days on the wrong side of the law, or commit any other crimes, must remember this: a criminal has to get away with every crime he or she commits. However, to get criminals off the street and put them behind bars, the police only have to catch a criminal once.

The methods by which police catch criminals are varied. Some are as old as recorded history and others are so new that they have yet to be tested in court. One of the first stories in the Bible is of murder, when Cain killed his brother Abel (Genesis 4:1–16). With few suspects to consider and an omniscient detective, this was an easy crime to solve. However, much later in that same work, a young man named Daniel steps in when a woman is accused of an immoral act by two elders (Daniel 13:1–63). By using the standard police practice of separating the witnesses before questioning them, he is able to arrive at the truth of the matter.

From the time of the Bible to almost present day, police investigations did not progress much further than questioning witnesses and searching the crime scene for obvious clues as to a criminal's identity. It was not until the late 1800s that science began to be employed. In 1879 the French began to use physical measurements and later photography to identify repeat offenders. In the same year a Scottish missionary in Japan used a handprint found on a wall to exonerate a man accused of theft. In 1892 a bloody fingerprint led Argentine police to charge and convict a mother of killing her children, and by 1905 Scotland Yard had convicted several criminals thanks to this new science.

Progress continued. By the 1920s scientists were using blood analysis to determine if recovered stains were from the victim or suspect, and the new field of firearms examination helped link bullets to the guns that fired them.

Nowadays, things are even harder on criminals, when by leaving behind a speck of blood, dropping a sweat-stained hat, or even taking a sip from a can of soda, they can give the police everything they need to identify and arrest them.

In the first decade of the twenty-first century the main tools used by the police include

- questioning witnesses and suspects
- searching the crime scene for physical evidence
- employing informants and undercover agents
- investigating the whereabouts of previous offenders when a crime they've been known to commit has occurred
- using computer databases to match evidence found on one crime scene to that found on others or to previously arrested suspects
- sharing information with other law enforcement agencies via the Internet
- using modern communications to keep the public informed and enlist their aid in ongoing investigations

But just as they have many different tools with which to solve crime, so too do they have many different kinds of crime and criminals to investigate. There is murder, kidnapping, and bank robbery. There are financial crimes committed by con men who gain their victim's trust or computer experts who hack into computers. There are criminals who have formed themselves into gangs and those who are organized into national syndicates. And there are those who would kill as many people as possible, either for the thrill of taking a human life or in the horribly misguided belief that it will advance their cause.

The Criminal Investigations series looks at all of the above and more. Each book in the series takes one type of crime and gives the reader an overview of the history of the crime, the methods and motives behind it, the people who have committed it, and the means by which these people are caught and punished. In this series celebrity crimes will be discussed and exposed. Mysteries that have yet to be solved will be presented. Readers will discover the truth about murderers, serial killers, and bank robbers whose stories have become myths and legends. These books will explain how criminals can separate a person from his hard-earned cash, how they prey on the weak and helpless, what is being done to stop them, and what one can do to help prevent becoming a victim.

John L. French,
Crime Scene Supervisor,
Baltimore Police Crime Laboratory

* Federal Bureau of Investigation. "Uniform Crime Reports, Crime in the United States 2000." Available online. URL: http://www.fbi.gov/ucr/00cius.htm. Accessed January 11, 2008.

Acknowledgments

The author gratefully acknowledges all of the persons who helped in the production of this book. Without their help it would have been impossible. Editor James Chambers, my agent Jake Elwell, private investigator Vincent Parco, my wife Lisa Grasso, Agnieszka Biegaj, Corporate Communications Officer of Europol; author David Henry Jacobs, Philip Semrau, Nathan Versace, Keith Brenner, Eddie and Cate Behringer, Larry Beck, Scott Frommer, and the Drug Enforcement Administration Museum in Arlington, Virginia.

Introduction:
Fighting Drugs Gets
Harder Every Day

Fighting the illegal drug trade is harder today than ever before. Drug traffickers work with state-of-the-art equipment and a streamlined, well-organized system to produce and distribute illegal drugs. Profits from drug sales keep them rich and powerful. Fortunately, law enforcement is keeping up. The techniques used to fight drugs are getting more sophisticated every day.

How did drug dealers get so much money? How did the drug barons become so powerful? There are a few reasons, including primarily the supply of drugs, and the demand for drugs.

One "supply" reason is that the production and sale of drugs is restricted by most governments. This creates a back market for drugs that drives the price of drugs sky high and funnels tremendous amounts of money into the pockets of drug dealers.[1] The "demand" reason has to do with the economic conditions around the globe. It is true that there is a lot of poverty in the world, but it is also true that more people have more money. There is a growing global middle class. They easily pay their rent or their mortgage each month. They have leisure time—and they have money to buy drugs. With both the supply of drugs and the demand for drugs on the rise, the law enforcement officers who are combating illegal drugs have their hands full.[2]

A third reason often goes unstated, and that is the War on Terror. Since 9/11 the United States and the world has increased its efforts in the fight against terror. Agencies like the Federal Bureau of Investigation (FBI) and Immigration and Customs Enforcement (ICE) have shifted their priorities and resources to protecting the country from terrorists. That means less money and fewer people are available to combat the illegal drug trade. This has made it easier for drug traffickers to do their job and for drug **barons** to become rich and powerful.

Yet the war on drugs goes on. Though diminished in size in recent years, the world's anti-drug forces work hard. Working as a team, the world's justice departments still catch drug criminals, see them tried, and put them in jail for a long time. Because drugs are produced and distributed across international borders, cooperation among law enforcement agencies in different nations is essential to combating the drug trade. This book is about that war on drugs. It will look at how drugs are produced, transported, and sold. It will examine the many methods police all over the world use to try to stop the flow of illegal drugs.

From Coast Guard helicopters chasing down speedboats crammed full of illegal drugs to police raids that expose drug-trafficking rings, from anti-smuggling tactics at airports and seaports to how drug-sniffing dogs are trained, *Drug Crime* covers all aspects of law enforcement's efforts to stop the illegal drug trade.

THE PROBLEMS WITH DRUGS

There are several reasons why it is important to stop the flow of drugs into the United States. Some are more obvious than others.

To begin, the money spent on drugs goes to drug barons who use the cash to pay for other crimes. The money might go toward bribes of police and government officials, toward the purchase of illegal weapons, or other criminal enterprises such as prostitution.

Drugs are addictive and physically and psychologically damaging. **Addicts**, persons who are hooked on drugs, are sometimes called **junkies**. They have a strong physical need for the drug to which they are addicted. It is like a hunger that needs to be fed on a regular basis. As a result, junkies are sometimes forced to steal and commit crimes for profit in order to buy drugs. If, for some reason, they cannot get the drug they need, they may experience **withdrawal**, a serious sickness. Junkies in need of a "fix"—a dose of their drug—become more and more desperate. They may be willing to steal or even hurt or kill someone in order to buy the drugs they need so badly.

If that isn't enough, drugs drain away at people's quality of life. Drugs take away a user's potential. A person who could have been a success in life may die of an overdose or become institutionalized due to damage to their body or mind from drug use. Drugs also take away the potential of the communities in which they are sold and used. Neighborhoods can turn from friendly and safe into frightening war zones when drug dealers and users take over the streets. Plus, people under the influence of drugs are more likely to hurt themselves or others in accidents, most notably car accidents.

CRIMINAL CONNECTIONS

Businessmen who deal in drugs are criminals. Because of this, drug trafficking is often intertwined with other forms of crime, especially organized crime and racketeering.

Here's how drug rings work. First, drugs are produced. They are grown if they are derived from chemicals found in plants. Other drugs must be made in a laboratory. Once the drug has been made it must be divided and transported to the places where it will be sold. In many cases these places are on the other side of the world from where the drug was produced. Drug shipments often take journeys that are thousands of miles long.

Once the drugs reach their locations, they are divided up again and sold to drug users by small-time drug dealers. Almost all drug operations are led by one person at the top: the drug baron. The great majority of the money stays at the top of the organization, in the drug baron's pockets.

Those drug barons are among the richest individuals in the world. With that money comes enormous power. In foreign lands, and also in the United States to some extent, that power is great. Governments that are corrupt and influenced by bribes from the drug barons won't do anything to stop the flow of drugs and money.

AMERICAN AGENTS ABROAD

American agents try to stop the flow of drugs, even in corrupt countries. This is a dangerous business. The agents usually operate in the country where the drug was produced, countries and regions that are most likely to be corrupt. There, agents encounter resistance not only from the drug traffickers but also from the local and national governments. The leaders of the nation may have been bribed by the baron, so they are not on the same side as the U.S. anti-drug agents. Once the proper palms have been greased, the drug barons are in charge.[3]

This meth lab discovered by deer hunters in an Iowa forest was later photographed by agents of the Iowa Department of Natural Resources' law enforcement bureau in 2006. *Drug Enforcement Administration*

Law enforcement agencies go about their War on Drugs in a variety of ways. The war today takes place all along the drug-trafficking route, from the nickel- and dime-bag dealers in public parks, to the drug barons in foreign countries who are more powerful in their nations than even their presidents.

Authorities attempt to stop the production of drugs by going to the source. Some drugs are found in plants. These include marijuana, the leaves of which are smoked. Law enforcement will try, whenever it can, to find and destroy marijuana plants that are still growing in the ground.

Other drugs, such as LSD and methamphetamine (crank, crystal meth), are made up of chemicals and are produced in a lab. It is up to law enforcement to find these labs and put them out of business.

SECURING BORDERS

To prevent illegal drugs, among other things, from entering the United States, airports and seaports are heavily staffed with security agents who do their best to make sure no drugs enter the country and seize many tons of drugs from would-be smugglers each year. One of the most effective tools used by law enforcement to find hidden drugs in packages entering the country are specially trained dogs. These drug-sniffing dogs—sometimes called "sniffers"—can find hidden drugs more efficiently than a small army of humans.

Some smugglers, usually low-paid employees working for drug barons, attempt to enter the country with drugs hidden inside their bodies. They are called "drug mules," and they often risk their lives to hide illegal drugs, although the authorities have methods for capturing them and recovering the evidence.

Anti-drug smuggling agents are posted at airports, seaports, and stops along U.S. borders with Mexico and Canada. It would be impossible to stop all of the drugs coming into the country, because there are too many places to enter. Security agents can't watch them all. The idea is to stop as many drug shipments as possible. Police want to make life as difficult as they can for drug smugglers.

Not all drug investigations in other countries are hindered by uncooperative governments. Often they are successful. In 2005 DEA agents broke up three major drug transportation rings. The simultaneous arrests covered all the stops the drugs made on their

way from the fields of Colombia to their distribution centers within the United States.[4]

SECONDARY DRUG CRIME

In addition to illegal drug production and **trafficking**, there is also secondary drug crime to be fought. This doesn't involve crimes committed by the drug traffickers, such as the production, transportation, and sale of drugs. This is low-level crime, street crime, which comes when those addicted to drugs lack the money to buy their next fix. They steal the money, maybe hurting somebody in the process. Stopping such drug-related crime is also at the top of law enforcement's priority list. Secondary drug crimes may also include crimes committed by one drug dealer against another while attempting to expand or protect his or her "turf."

Ride along with law enforcement and the military as they bust smugglers and pushers. Learn how some smugglers hide drugs inside their own bodies, and how customs officials catch them. Follow the training step-by-step as drug-sniffing dogs and their trainers prepare to bust crime. Visit the dangerous world of moles and informants who risk their lives to gather evidence against drug distributors. And learn how technology has given law enforcement a boost through the development of futuristic electronic surveillance. Next stop: the front lines in the War on Drugs.

It Takes a Team

The battle against drugs is waged by an international *team* of law enforcement agents from many different agencies, representing many countries. There are police of every type: local police, state police, federal agents, customs and border patrol. There are investigators of every sort, even scientists, who work in a laboratory rather than out in the field. These are investigators who use a microscope and chemicals to find the evidence that puts drug barons and smugglers in prison.

BREAKING DOWN BORDERS

There was a time, not that long ago, when this sort of international teamwork simply did not exist. Each law enforcement agency had its own turf, called its **jurisdiction**. Each agency was powerless beyond its own borders. It was easy for organized drug criminals to avoid arrest and prosecution by avoiding jurisdictions where they were wanted by the police.

In today's world, law enforcement agents must be free to cross borders in the pursuit of drug criminals. Or they must be confident that there are agents on the other side of that border, ready and able to take up the chase.

There is a need for cooperation between various agencies and between the law enforcement officers of different countries. In Europe two international police forces fight drugs. They are Europol and Interpol. Their jurisdiction is not affected by the borders between countries. They can work in many different countries at the same time, and they can also help the police agencies in those various countries work together.

No such international force exists in North America, although there are task forces set up among Canada, Mexico, and the United States. These task forces work together to help halt the flow of drugs across the many thousands of miles of border that the countries of North America share. When it comes to criminal investigations, it is best if borders are all but erased.

OPERATION NORTHERN IMPACT

In the modern battle against drugs, law enforcement agencies have learned to work together. Take, for example, Operation Northern Impact in 2005. This investigation lasted two years and dismantled an entire cocaine trafficking operation.

The team in this case consisted of eight law enforcement agencies: the Drug Enforcement Administration (DEA), the Los Angeles District Attorney's Office, the California Highway Patrol, the Los Angeles Police Department (LAPD), the North Carolina State Police, the Greensboro (North Carolina) Police Department, the Arizona Department of Public Safety, and the Phoenix (Arizona) Police Department. The DEA expanded its investigatory ability by enlisting help from regional law enforcement agencies. Teaming up with local and state law enforcement agencies allowed the federal agency to be far more effective and efficient.

These agencies, when working together, made up what was called the Organized Crime Drug Enforcement Task Force. According to the DEA's Public Affairs Office, the operation "targeted an international cocaine and marijuana trafficking ring whose operations ranged across the Southwest Border and into the Northeastern United States. Operation *Northern Impact* resulted in the arrest of fifty-three individuals. The seizures . . . totaled 341 kilograms of cocaine, 2,258 pounds of marijuana, and $1.4 million in U.S. assets."[1]

About the successful conclusion of the investigation, DEA deputy administrator Michele M. Leonhart said that the busted traffickers had a network that "spanned our nation, ravaged our communities, and left countless lives grasping for hope from the tragedy of addiction." She said the operation had been proof of the DEA's "unwavering commitment to take dealers off the streets and drugs out of America's bloodstream."[2]

U.S. COAST GUARD

Although the United States Coast Guard serves a wide variety of functions, investigating crimes is one of its most important. In the War on Drugs, the Coast Guard is an important member of the team. Some Coast Guard officers are specially trained to be criminal investigators on anti-smuggling missions. This was why the Coast Guard was so quick to adapt to anti-terror efforts following the tragic events of 9/11. The methods used to combat terror and drugs are very similar.

The arm of the Coast Guard in charge of drug-smuggling prevention is called the U.S. Coast Guard (USCG) Drug Interdiction. It is

U.S. Coast Guard crewmembers guard bags containing more than one ton of cocaine in Miami Beach on February 16, 2006. *AP Photo/ Alan Diaz*

part of the USCG Office of Law Enforcement. The Coast Guard, along with the U.S. Customs Service, is responsible for combating the flow of illegal drugs into the United States. According to the Coast Guard, its mission is to "reduce the supply of drugs from the source by denying smugglers the use of air and maritime routes. . . ." The Coast Guard patrols many waters, including those of the Caribbean, the Gulf of Mexico, and the Eastern Pacific off the West Coast of the United States.[3]

The Coast Guard does not need daylight to spot a drug-smuggling boat. Coast Guard personnel have ways of "seeing" even when it is dark. One is night-vision glasses, which register the infrared waves given off by heat. People and motor engines are easily seen, no matter how dark it is. They also see objects using radar, a system that sends out radio waves, which hit objects such as boats and planes, and bounce back. By measuring the returning waves, Coast Guard anti-drug officers can tell how large a vehicle is, the direction it is headed, and how fast it is going.[4]

U.S. CUSTOMS BUREAU

United States Customs agents work at the nation's various ports of entry. It doesn't make any difference if someone enters the country by land, sea, or air. Everyone must pass through customs first. Customs agents are posted at seaports, airports, and at major roads that cross the border. In countries where drugs are produced, customs officials are also concerned with drugs leaving the country.

Customs officials have the right to search individuals, vehicles, and packages. The searches are often done in a random fashion, but particular people and items may be singled out for search if anything about the situation strikes the agent as suspicious. Customs officials can't search the person and luggage of every tourist who attempts to enter the country. Some people are searched and some aren't. Some of the things customs officers look for when determining whom to search are

- sweaty hands
- fast breathing
- indications of nervousness and/or deception
- inappropriate clothing
- signs of physical discomfort such as abdominal cramping

- travel route, such as passengers arriving on planes and ships from countries known to produce and export illegal drugs
- anxiety
- rushed behavior
- evidence of alcohol or drug use

In order to know where to post themselves to best fight drug smuggling, customs officials rely on the cooperation of other

A U.S. Customs Service police officer examines some of the 163 toothpaste tubes containing cocaine seized from a Haitian woman arriving at Miami International Airport on March 13, 2001. *AP Photo/ U.S. Customs Service*

organizations. These include the military and intelligence services—the FBI or CIA, for example—who may have unearthed evidence regarding drug trafficking while fighting terror or spying on enemies.[5]

FORENSIC SCIENTISTS: IMPORTANCE OF TRACE EVIDENCE

Another key member of the team is the forensic scientist. He or she works in a laboratory and uses chemical tests to detect very small amounts of illegal drugs, called trace evidence, on various items. These might include

- clothes a suspect was wearing
- a weapon
- money
- a residence

The newest type of forensic scientists are DNA specialists. DNA is a chemical code present in every cell in one's body that, when identified in a lab, can be matched against cells left behind in the form of hair, skin, saliva, and other bodily fluids. DNA evidence can be used to link a suspect with a crime scene. In the case of a violent crime, DNA can link criminals with their victims. In some cases DNA can match the suspect to the seized drugs.[6]

TESTING FOR DRUGS

Forensic scientists use several methods to determine if submitted evidence is comprised of or contains illegal drugs. These tools are powerful microscopes, chemicals, and a machine called the "shake and vac."

The shake and vac finds traces of illegal drugs on currency—or any other item that can be shaken. The process is simple. The currency is shaken in a clean container so that all particles clinging to it fall off. The area is then vacuumed and the gathered material is tested for drugs. The shake and vac can also find evidence that links the money to the criminals who handled it. There have been cases when a hair or a thread found inside a sample of drugs can, through microscope analysis, lead to the guilty party or parties being arrested.[7]

CHROMATOGRAPHY

Chromatography is a useful testing method to determine if a substance is, or contains, an illegal drug. According to the Rensselaer Polytechnic Institute, the United States' oldest technological university, **chromatography** is "a broad range of physical methods used to separate and or to analyze complex mixtures." In other words, substances are mixed with a second substance, called a **reagent**.

An agent with the South Carolina Law Enforcement's Forensic Science Division uses gas chromatography and mass spectrometry to fingerprint different drugs taken from a biosample in January 2005. AP Photo/Mary Ann Chastain

This causes the substance to separate by color. The color pattern that is produced identifies what the substance is.

For example, the test to determine if LSD is present is called the Van Urk test. When mixed with a reagent, a sample will turn blue if LSD is present.

A similar test for heroin is called the Marquis test. When mixed with its reagent, the sample containing heroin turns purple.

℗ ILLEGAL DRUGS AT A GLANCE

The Controlled Substances Act, passed into law in 1970, gives the government the authority to classify and control various substances according to their medical usefulness and risk for abuse and addiction. The Drug Schedule includes five main categories. Schedule I drugs are those considered the most addictive and dangerous and which have few or no accepted medical uses. The lowest risk drugs with legitimate medical applications fall into Schedule V, and Schedule II through IV covers the range of drugs in between. For more details about the Controlled Substances Act, the Drug Schedule, and types of drugs, go online to http://www. usdoj.gov/dea/pubs/abuse/1-csa.htm and http://www.usdoj.gov/ dea/pubs/scheduling.html.

Here's a quick rundown of the types of illegal drugs law enforcement is combating.

- *Marijuana (herb, grass, Mary Jane, pot, weed)*. A plant, the leaves of which are smoked, or sometimes eaten, to get high (a relaxed and dreamy state). The chemical in the plant that causes the high is called THC.
- *LSD (acid)* is a hallucinogenic chemical. Very small amounts enable the user to "take a trip," which is to experience hallucinations and sensory changes. Users may see or hear things that are not really there. LSD, which is swallowed, may also cause users to lose touch with reality. Drastic mood swings are common. Other **hallucinogens** include mescaline and magic mushrooms, or "shrooms."
- *Cocaine (coke, blow, snow)* is a chemical derived from the leaf of the coca plant. It may be ground into a fine powder and sniffed up the nose, or heated into a liquid and injected with a

The test itself can be as simple as putting droplets of the sample on a test strip to see if the strip changes color.[8]

MASS SPECTROMETRY

Another method of identifying unknown substances is called mass spectrometry. It has an advantage over chromatography in

syringe. Today it is also smoked, particularly as crack cocaine, which is very potent. It is a powerful stimulant that also kills pain and is highly addictive. Most of the cocaine that enters the United States comes from South America.

■ *Vicodin, Codeine,* and *Heroin (H, smack, horse, junk)* are all drugs called opiates, because they are based on opium, a drug produced from the poppy plant. The drugs are high-powered painkillers. Another opiate, morphine, is used by the military in wartime to treat the pain of the severely wounded. The dulling of the senses makes the person less aware and more carefree. Opiates are very addictive. Once hooked, stopping usage of an opiate can cause the drug addict to have severely painful withdrawal symptoms. Opiates can be taken orally, snorted through the nose, or injected with a syringe. Addicts who inject heroin directly into their veins are called mainliners.

■ *Ecstasy (X, XTC, Pills, Rolls, E-tarts, ADAM, Go, Speed for LOV-ERS, Love Drug, Hug Drug, Scooby Snacks)* and other *amphetamines (speed, ups)* are stimulants. They make a person high and energized, often without the need of sleep for long stretches. When the effects wear off, the person will feel sick with fatigue, often causing the user to take the drug again, thus starting a vicious circle. Ecstasy causes people to lose their inhibitions and is popular in the club scene.

■ *Depressants*, such as *barbiturates (downers, goof balls)*, cause the user to slow down, become sleepy, and feel less angry and tense. They are legal when prescribed by a doctor, and become illegal only when used without a doctor's permission.

that only a very small amount of the substance is needed for the test to be successful. According to the American Society for Mass Spectrometry, scientists identify substances by observing their molecular structure through molecular microscopes. Not only is a very small sample necessary, but it is impossible to hide the substance by mixing it with something else. For example, one grain of cocaine dissolved in a quart of water would be easily identified using mass spectrometry.[9]

Military Operations

It was early 2003 and Lieutenants Craig Neubecker, William Greer, and Shawn Koch of the U.S. Coast Guard were climbing into their MH-68 Stingray helicopter. The helicopter was sitting on the flight deck of the Coast Guard cutter *Diligence*. (A cutter is any Coast Guard boat that is longer than 60 feet.) The 210-foot cutter was cruising off the western Central American coast.

Neubecker had already had a noteworthy career in the service. In December 2000 he had been involved in the daring rescue of 34 crewmembers from the disabled ship *Sea Breeze I*, sinking off the coast of Virginia. That incident became the subject of a Discovery Channel special and an *ABC Primetime Live* episode.

On this night the *Diligence* was on patrol in a well-known drug-transit zone of the Eastern Pacific Ocean about 250 miles west of Costa Rica. The 210-foot Coast Guard cutter is the smallest boat in the U.S. military to come with its own helipad, a flat area from which helicopters can take off and land. In the helicopter, Neubecker was the pilot, Koch was the co-pilot, and Greer was the gunner.[1]

The Stingray could do more than chase down a boat trying to smuggle drugs. If the smugglers fired at the chopper, the chopper could return fire.[2] There were also machine guns and rifles for the crew to choose from. Neubecker later told the story of what happened next to the Cowley College Alumni Newsletter. He said:

> In the late evening, the *Diligence* received an intelligence report of a 'go-fast' drug-smuggling vessel in the area. Go-fasts are high-speed, multi-engined boats usually carrying several tons of illegal cargo. Unfortunately, the darkness and prevailing weather at the time meant detection of the go-fast would

This Coast Guard cutter, the type of ship used to pursue drug smugglers at sea, is equipped with a helipad. *Drug Enforcement Administration*

be nearly impossible, and up to that time, not a single go-fast had been stopped at night.[3]

It wasn't a good night to go hunting speedboats racing across the ocean. The sky was overcast, with clouds at 700 feet. Visibility was only one mile. It was raining off and on. The Coast Guard would have to rely on night-vision glasses and radar to spot the drug-smuggling boat.[4]

Was it an impossible mission? Neubecker weighed all of the factors and decided the answer was no. The information they had received was good. Here was a chance to do their job. They would at least have to try.

The Stingray tracked the go-fast boat as it sped toward the U.S. shore. Greer fired warning shots over the speedboat's bow, hoping that the smugglers could be stopped in the water without further

⚲ HOW DRUGS ARE "CUT"

In order to increase profits, dealers mix pure drugs they have received from their suppliers with other substances to create the illusion that there is more of the drug than there actually is. For example, a dealer may receive a delivery of one kilogram of pure cocaine. The dealer will then mix that drug with three kilograms of some other inexpensive white powder. He then divides the resulting substance into bags containing smaller quantities and sells them as if they were pure cocaine, and at the price of pure cocaine. In reality, the content of each bag is only one-quarter cocaine, and the dealer has multiplied his profits by four.

violence. The boat continued to speed along. Greer's next shots had to be precise. They were designed to stop the boat without injuring anyone aboard. Using the helicopter's .50-caliber precision rifle, Greer disabled the go-fast boat's engines with pinpoint shots. Dead in the water, the speedboat's crew and cargo were captured.

The mission resulted in the seizure of more than three tons of uncut (that is, pure and undiluted) cocaine with a street value of more than $194 million from reaching the United States. That was three tons that would never reach the streets. Along with the drugs, the Coast Guard also seized the drug smugglers' outboard motors, weapons, and ammunition.

Neubecker later commented:

It was without a doubt the most difficult mission I have ever flown. And while many have praised us for completing the mission, some have also questioned why we even tried it. The simple answer is that it is our duty, and we must all do our part to serve our country, just like our other brothers and sisters in arms serving around the world are doing their part.

For their work on this mission, Neubecker and Greer were awarded the Airborne Law Enforcement Association's 2003–2004 Captain "Gus" Crawford Memorial Air Crew of the Year Award.[5]

The number-one force fighting drug smugglers entering the United States by boat is the U.S. Coast Guard. As part of what the Coast Guard calls their drug-interdiction program, it uses its vessels to spot and stop smugglers. The United States has thousands of miles of coastline and the Coast Guard does its best to keep an eye on all of it. Naturally they focus most of their attention on locations where drug traffickers are most apt to try to get their drugs ashore. These locations include San Francisco Bay, New York Harbor, and the Florida Everglades.

THE NAVY AND THE WAR ON DRUGS

Like the Coast Guard, the navy takes an active role to prevent drug smugglers, also called drug runners, from using the waters around the United States as a route to bring drugs into the United States. The U.S. armed forces are limited in their ability to fight the War on Drugs by the Posse Comitatus laws that prohibit the military from acting as police in the United States. However, the 1989 National Defense Authorization Act allows naval vessels to support Coast Guard anti-drug smuggling operations on the high seas.

Tasks undertaken by navy ships include patrolling and investigating any suspicious looking boats or ships. On occasions when the navy makes drug arrests, prisoners are turned over to the Coast Guard.

⚲ SATELLITE SURVEILLANCE

Today's drug smugglers have to worry about more than undercover agents with hidden microphones and cameras. Today, the movements of drug traffickers can be watched from ships far off shore and even by satellites hundreds of miles up in space. Modern **surveillance** satellites transmit their images to receivers on Earth without delay. If the satellite shows a drug-smuggling boat heading for shore, the images will arrive in time for the authorities to do something about it. The cameras on the satellites are so good that photos taken from space are clear enough that license plates can be read.[6]

Although most of the drugs entering the United States from Mexico arrive over land, there are many instances of drug runners trying to transport their drugs by boat. These journeys usually start on the west coast of Mexico and head northward, usually landing somewhere along the California coast.

In July 2004 the USS *Crommelin* and the USS *Ticonderoga* were patrolling the waters of the eastern Pacific when they spotted a speedboat, still miles from shore, racing toward the land at breakneck speed. The boat's crew refused to identify itself and ignored orders to halt. In order to prevent the boat from making it to shore, teamwork was again in order—the two navy ships had to work together.

According to the navy Web site, "With USS *Crommelin* acting as a blocker, USS *Ticonderoga* maneuvered ahead of a speedboat and ordered the drug runners to stop. USS *Ticonderoga* performed all the necessary steps to persuade the speedboat to halt."

Using a Forward Looking Infrared (FLIR) camera, a camera that sees heat rather than light, crewmembers saw and recorded the speedboat's crew throwing their illegal cargo overboard. USS *Ticonderoga* then broke from the chase to recover the contraband while USS *Crommelin* continued pursuit and intercepted the speedboat. USS *Ticonderoga* recovered 72 cocaine bales weighing 50 pounds each and worth $36 million street value. The smugglers were all captured and turned over to the Coast Guard.[7]

THE U.S. ARMY VS. MANUEL NORIEGA

The U.S. Army also plays a role in anti-drug efforts. One action undertaken by the military as part of the War on Drugs was the 1989 invasion of Panama. The operation, code-named Operation Just Cause, involved 25,000 U.S. troops. The United States claimed that General Manuel Noriega, head of the Panamanian government, was involved in drug trafficking. Their information came from several low-ranking drug runners and one Panamanian diplomat named Ricardo Bilonik, who agreed to provide evidence against Noriega. Noriega's position as the country's leader made it next to impossible to stop the flow of cocaine from Panama into the United States. The United States couldn't get Panamanian police to arrest Noriega because Noriega controlled them. The only solution was to use the U.S. Army, which invaded Panama and overthrew Noriega's

An American soldier sits in his foxhole in the Panamanian jungle in December 1989 during Operation Just Cause. *Les Stone/Sygma/Corbis*

government. He was replaced by politicians more cooperative with the U.S.'s anti-drug efforts. Noriega was brought to the United States where he was tried and convicted on drug charges and sentenced to 40 years in prison.[8]

Another military action taken as part of the War on Drugs was Plan Colombia, which was a fine example of international teamwork. In Plan Columbia, both military and private planes were used to poison the coca fields in Colombia. The U.S. military was also used to train the Colombian armed forces in how to eradicate—that is, wipe out—the coca fields. Plan Colombia

A Colombian soldier flees after a cocaine laboratory is destroyed as a part of Plan Colombia. *Reuters/Corbis*

was originally the idea of Colombian President Andres Pastrana Arango, and included U.S. financial aid to that country to boost Colombia's economy. The spraying of poisons in the fields to kill the coca plants was the most controversial aspect of the plan, however, because the herbicides, chemicals used to kill the plants, also hurt legal crops and had health effects on the people in the affected regions.[9]

Through the Air

There was a time, 50 years ago, when smuggling drugs into the United States by airplane was the method favored by drug traffickers, but, because of changes made in the law and law enforcement, that is no longer the case.

In the late 1960s the U.S. Congress responded to the growing number of airborne smugglers by establishing the Customs Air Program, which became operational in 1971. The program used surplus military reconnaissance planes and helicopters to reduce the flow of drugs across U.S. borders by air, and to help other anti-smuggling organizations with their efforts.[1]

During the 1970s the program received additional funding and adopted state-of-the-art technology, such as the most modern radar and other surveillance equipment. In response, smugglers who at one time would have flown across the border, landed in the United States, and unloaded their cargo, now had to change their strategy. Smugglers began to airdrop their cargo to boats waiting off shore.[2]

Customs Air Program aircraft also helped battle drugs in other ways besides detecting suspicious aircraft. When customs officials stop a land vehicle they suspect of carrying drugs, they let the vehicle through rather than bust its occupants. Customs aircraft then follow the suspicious truck to its destination in hopes of making an even larger bust when the smugglers meet their dealers.[3]

Today, because of these and similar efforts, air smuggling is no longer as prevalent as it was, but it is not completely gone, especially in other countries.

During the spring of 2006 Mexican soldiers seized five and a half tons of cocaine worth more than $100 million from a commercial plane arriving from Venezuela. The seizure took place at the airport of Ciudad de Carmen, 550 miles east of Mexico City, after the

Mexican military received information from Venezuelan and U.S. authorities.

According to a statement made by Mexico's Defense Department, the cocaine was stacked in 128 black suitcases marked "Private."[4] The pilot escaped, but the co-pilot was arrested. There were no passengers. Two men at the airport who were waiting with another airplane were also arrested. The second airplane was believed to be ready to take the drugs to its next location.

Officials in the United States and Mexico believe the amount of cocaine and heroin passing from Colombia through Venezuela to Mexico, where it is smuggled into the United States, is increasing. While drug traffickers used planes to smuggle large quantities of drugs in the 1990s, most Mexican traffickers now use land and sea routes. Venezuela became a key transit point for drugs because of, according to the U.S. State Department, "rampant corruption at the highest levels of law enforcement and a weak judicial system." So, smugglers use the skies, as well as land and water, to transport drugs, but law enforcement agencies are airborne too.[5]

COAST GUARD AIRCRAFT

The Coast Guard uses aircraft as well as watercraft to detect and stop the smuggling of drugs into the United States. The three types of craft most commonly used by the Coast Guard for this purpose are

- The HU-25 Falcon, a small airplane used for surveillance. It can fly very low over the ground or water, enabling Coast Guard personnel to see objects below.
- The HH-68A Stingray, a 44-foot helicopter equipped with machine guns and rifles. This is the type of chopper flown by Lieutenant Greer to track down a drug-packed speedboat in 2003, as discussed in Chapter 2. The Coast Guard uses this helicopter to locate drug smugglers on the ground and, if necessary, engage them. In other words, if the drug smugglers shoot at the helicopter, the Coast Guardsmen can shoot back.[6]
- AWACS. The Airborne Warning and Control System is a sophisticated surveillance system. Planes equipped with AWACS can spot "fast boats" smuggling drugs from 25,000 feet in the air.[7]

An air-to-air view of an E-3A Sentry aircraft equipped with AWACS, a valuable tool for detecting drug smugglers. *Getty Images*

DUSTING THE CROPS

Police also try to combat drug production from the air. One way is by flying over drug crops—such as marijuana, coca plants, or poppy fields—and spraying poisons on the plants to kill them.

This method punishes the farmers growing the plants as much as the drug barons who profit from the drugs those crops would produce. The poison raids, conducted with propeller planes and helicopters, are generally successful, but pilots often have to fly through gunfire from the ground as the farmers and agents of the drug barons shoot at them.

⚲ THE 9/11 EFFECT

The events of September 11, 2001, had a major effect on efforts to stop the flow of drugs into the United States. The meaning of "protecting our borders" changed that day. U.S. national security authorities stopped thinking of the borders as a place to prevent drug smuggling, and began thinking in terms of the War on Terror. Drugs that might otherwise have been stopped at the borders were now going to get through because the Border Patrol and other border security personnel were going to be spending most of their time and energy trying to prevent further terrorist attacks. One example of this is how canine detectives are trained. Dogs that were once trained to sniff out drugs in airports and harbors are now trained to sniff out explosives. Not all of the news is bad, however. The budget for protecting U.S. borders has risen, and increased security has had the collateral effect, in many cases, of making drug smuggling more difficult.[8]

To further hinder the drug barons without hurting the farmers, who were generally poor and just trying to get by, the anti-drug forces tried a little bribe of their own: They offered to pay farmers in drug-producing countries to grow crops other than drug crops. For example, farmers who grew coffee instead of marijuana received payments from the government.

The plan did not work. Farmers rejected the deal because the bribes weren't big enough. The farmers could still make more money growing the drug-producing crops than they could growing something legitimate. Plus, even in cases where anti-drug agents were generous enough to make it worthwhile for the farmers to switch crops, the farmers feared reprisal from the drug barons and refused to take the anti-drug money. And, human nature being what it is, some farmers no doubt took the bribes then continued to grow illegal drugs.[9]

What's a
Drug Mule?

Sometimes drug traffickers use commercial airliners to smuggle their products. In these cases they often use a "drug mule" to do the dirty work for them. A drug mule is the person who actually smuggles the drugs. The drugs may be hidden in the drug mule's luggage or clothing.

One of the largest Ecstasy busts ever came in 2001 in a Japanese airport when a Russian man carrying a fake Israeli passport tried to enter Japan. Security first noticed the man because his clothes seemed too bulky for August. He was strip searched and found to have 30,000 Ecstasy, also called "X," tablets hidden on his body. He also carried two suitcases. Each suitcase had a false bottom. In the hidden compartment were tens of thousands of Ecstasy tablets. The two suitcases combined contained 23,000 tablets. Altogether he was trying to smuggle 53,000 hits of X.[1]

Women pretending to be pregnant have also tried to fool keen-eyed customs agents at international airports. When these women are searched it turns out that they are not expecting a baby at all, but rather are wearing a body suit filled with drugs under their clothes.

The most notorious drug mules, though, don't hide the drugs under their clothes or in their luggage. They hide the drugs inside their bodies. This is accomplished in two ways. One method is to wrap the drugs in balloons, condoms, latex gloves, or plastic bags, then swallow them so that the drug mule carries the package inside his or her stomach. The digestive system will not break down the wrapping right away, allowing the drugs to pass through the mule's body when he or she has reached his or her destination. The other method is to insert the plastic bags up the rectum, so that they are carried inside the colon. Both methods are unpleasant and risky.

DRUG MULES AS VICTIMS

Being a drug mule can be very dangerous. Drug barons use mules because the method greatly reduces the chances that they themselves or their regular agents will be caught.

Becoming a drug mule is the occupation of someone who is truly desperate. During the late spring of 2004 an 82-year-old woman flying from Bogota to the United States had a devastating stomachache after she arrived at JFK Airport in New York City. She died before an ambulance could get her to a hospital. An autopsy revealed that the woman had died of a drug overdose, after a rubber bag full of narcotics broke in her stomach. Reporters learned that the woman had been working as a drug mule to make enough money to secure the future of her adult son, who was mentally handicapped and unable to take care of himself.

That same year a mother and her 16-year-old son, both serving as drug mules, arrived in New York. Their trip took a tragic turn on the way to a nearby hotel in Queens when a rubber bag burst in the boy's stomach, releasing the drugs it contained. The boy's mother left the young man to die in the hotel room.[2]

Sometimes animals are used as drug mules. On February 1, 2006, the DEA released a troubling story: John P. Gilbride, the special agent-in-charge of the New York Field Division of the DEA announced that 20 Colombian nationals had been arrested for smuggling 20 kilograms of heroin into the United States through New York's JFK Airport. In addition to the human smugglers, there were purebred puppies with heroin packets surgically implanted in them. In one instance, six puppies were found impregnated with a total of 3 kilograms of liquid heroin in packets. The heroin was also concealed in body creams, aerosol cans, and pressed into small balls then sewn into the lining of purses and double-sided luggage.[3] Gilbride said:

> The organization's outrageous and heinous smuggling method of implanting heroin inside puppies is a true indication of the

USING X-RAYS TO CATCH MULES

If a person attempting to enter the country is suspected of being a drug mule, officials may use an X-ray machine at the airport or ship port to determine on the spot if the suspect is hiding illegal

(continues)

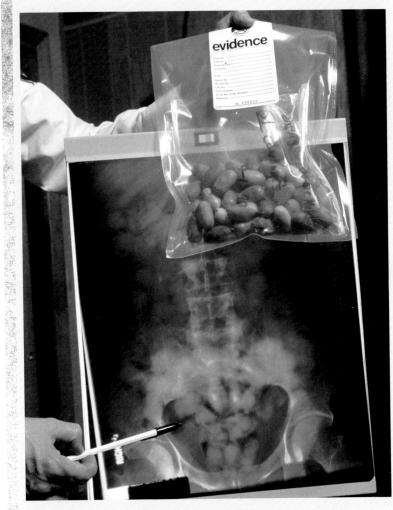

An airport customs agent shows an X-ray of a drug mule's stomach along with the drugs recovered from the person's body.
Jacques M. Chenet/Corbis

(continued)

substances in his or her body. According to the Department of Radiology at Feldkirch Hospital in Feldkirch, Austria, radiologists (doctors who take and interpret X-rays) must know some simple rules to correctly identify drugs inside a person's body. They are

- Hashish is denser than stool.
- Cocaine appears similar to stool.
- Heroin is slightly transparent and may appear on an X-ray like a foggy gas.

The easiest way to identify drugs in an X-ray is by the packages that contain them. Rubber bags or latex gloves that have been swallowed or inserted are more uniform in shape and have a smoother surface than the ordinary contents of the stomach or intestines.

extent that drug dealers go to make their profit. This investigation identified the individuals who were responsible for overseeing and smuggling millions of dollars worth of heroin from Colombia to the East Coast.

There were 14 separate seizures of heroin totaling 24 kilograms, one seizure of 6 kilograms of cocaine, and 22 arrests in the puppy case. These arrests came after a two-year, multi-agency investigation that identified an organization based in Medellin, Colombia, whose distribution network reached from Miami to New York City.[4]

SPECIAL TOILETS

Only a small percentage of the drug mules who attempt to enter the country die of an overdose, but a significant number experience some physical discomfort. The discomfort can be enough for a keen-eyed security officer to spot and start asking questions. If the answers do not suit the security officer, the subject may be given an invasive body-cavity search.[5]

This January 2005 photo shows a Colombian policeman holding a dog with a scar on its stomach where drug smugglers had surgically inserted heroin. *Albeiro Lopera/Reuters/Corbis*

On other occasions, the security officer's eyes don't need to be so keen.

In 2006 the cable news network MSNBC reported:

> During fiscal year 2003 there were 106 seizures of heroin at JFK Airport alone, equaling 237 pounds, and 32 seizures of cocaine equaling 63 pounds. Drug mules usually carry about two pounds of narcotics in 18 to 25 pellets. A pellet consists of a condom or latex glove stuffed with the drugs.[6]

According to one DEA official:

> In order to assist in the difficult process of swallowing the illicit cargo, drug mules are usually given substances such as Chloraseptic to loosen up and numb the throat. Heroin is often smuggled by people who swallow large numbers of small capsules—fifty to ninety—allowing them to transport up to one and a half kilograms of heroin per courier.[7]

It is an extremely unpleasant business to arrest a drug mule attempting to enter the country and then try to recover the evidence. Cutting the person open and pulling the drugs out is not an option. In most cases the drugs come out naturally. If the drugs are deep enough into the colon, a body-cavity search won't uncover them. Stronger methods must be used.

Therefore, security stations near common entry points into the country are equipped with special toilets, which can be used to recover drugs from the mules. Officials give the mules medications to induce vomiting or diarrhea and force the drugs to pass from the mule's system.

The toilets are inside a small stall with frosted glass walls. When the toilet is flushed the matter doesn't go into the sewer system, but rather through a glass tube and into a metal and glass cabinet inside a laboratory. Scientists then search through the matter, using a high-powered spray of water to separate the bags of drugs from the feces.

Recovering the drugs must be done quickly. The acids and digestive juices in a person's stomach can eat a hole in a latex glove or condom. Once the drugs start to escape into the drug mule's digestive system, the person is in agony. Seizures then occur as the drug mule overdoses, and the exposure can be fatal.[8]

OTHER HIDING PLACES

Drug smugglers rely on the fact that people travel with a lot of containers in their luggage. Even in the post-9/11 era, airport and seaport security cannot open every container of deodorant, shaving cream, toothpaste, or other common items to see what is inside. Therefore, placing drugs inside containers that are unlikely to be opened has proved successful as a smuggling method. Putting drugs inside a can of shaving cream could work, because it is unlikely that security will break open the can. If they check at all, they may only squirt out a little of the shaving cream to make sure the can actually contains shaving cream. Only a small amount of shaving cream needs to be inside the can. The rest of the can could be jam-packed with illegal drugs.

Not all drug smugglers who use clever containers avoid capture and punishment. Sergeant Jose Luis Queija of the Guardia Civil anti-narcotics squad at Barajas Airport in Madrid, Spain, has a collection of containers that have been found to contain drugs. Among these are a bowling ball, a bottle of shaving cream, statuettes, liquor bottles, wheelchairs, bicycles, animal cages, and tropical fruits. He thinks the cleverest hiding place might have been the smuggler who put his drugs inside the stems of carnations.[9]

Especially smart drug smugglers will often use containers that don't appear to be containers. Drugs could be stored in the hollowed-out heels of a pair of shoes, for example. Heroin could be

♀ DON'T BE AN ACCIDENTAL MULE

If a stranger asked someone to swallow 50 condoms filled with white powder, that person would get suspicious. But it is important never to even carry someone else's bags or belongings across a border. In 2005 a Bahraini man in Indonesia was found to be carrying oranges that were filled with more than juice and pulp. They contained heroin. The man said he was carrying the oranges for a friend and immediately gave up his friend's name. It turned out the man carrying the oranges was innocent, but he spent time in jail before the police were able to verify his story.

hidden inside plastic religious figurines, or cocaine could enter the country packed inside a box of hollowed-out Bibles.

Drug smugglers use new methods all the time, so security officers must constantly be alert for new ways to hide drugs as they enter the country. In a 2006 New York City bust, plastic envelopes filled with marijuana were found inside radio-controlled toys, in the compartment where the batteries would normally be.[10]

FLIGHT CREW ON THE ALERT

There was a time when the pilot and crew on commercial airliners simply flew the plane and took care of the passengers, but those days are long gone. The crews on today's commercial flights also double as security and anti-smuggling personnel.

Flight attendants screen passengers for suspicious behavior. They look for inappropriate clothes, because couriers will often wear too much clothing or bulky clothing to disguise the fact that they are hiding packages on their person. Flight crews will also make note of anyone who shows signs of digestive stress, cramping, stomachaches, or any discomfort in the midsection. That's because these signs may indicate someone is a drug mule.

Once identified by the flight crew, these passengers may be detained when they arrive at the airport. They may be strip-searched, or they may be examined to determine if they have drugs hidden inside their body.

THE NOSE KNOWS

Another method of smuggling drugs is to dissolve the drugs in water, soak and saturate clothing in the solution, and then after the clothes dry, bring them across the border. Once the drug mule is safely in the country the process is reversed, and the drugs are leeched out of the clothing and reconstituted. (To accomplish this, the clothes are washed with hot water only, no soap, and the "dirty" water is collected and allowed to evaporate, leaving the drugs behind.) Such a scheme would seem difficult to stop, but such smuggling techniques have proven vulnerable to the anti-drug agent's best friend, the drug-sniffing dog.

At JFK Airport during the 1990s, a drug-sniffing dog picked out 38 women's dresses shipped into the country from Bolivia. The dresses were taken to a lab where chemical tests determined that the cloth contained cocaine. The cocaine was removed from the cloth through a washing and evaporation process. An amazing 13 pounds of coke were recovered with a street value at the time of more than $1 million.

Informants

An informant is someone inside a criminal organization, or with knowledge of that organization, who tells police what they know about a criminal enterprise. The information is generally given in exchange for something. In cases where the informant is wanted for a crime, the reward could be a shorter prison sentence or no prison sentence at all. It may be immunity from prosecution for their part in the crimes about which they inform. In cases in which informants are not wanted for criminal activity, they are often given money or other considerations in exchange for the information they supply. Using informants, law enforcement authorities can break entire drug-trafficking operations.

In most cases it works like this: A low-level member of the crime organization is arrested. A deal is made and the arrested person agrees to inform on his bosses in the crime ring in exchange for a short jail term. The boss is then arrested and urged to inform on his boss, and so on, and so on. If everything goes the way police want it to, they can arrest everyone right up to the boss of bosses, the drug baron.

In the 1970s Drug Enforcement Administration (DEA) agents, using a series of paid informants and good old-fashioned spying, busted the major suppliers of heroin to Kansas City, Missouri. Agents had previously busted a Kansas City drug ring in 1974 called the Black Mafia, an organized crime group comprised of African Americans. But within a couple of years the supply of heroin was once again flowing freely in the area and DEA agents needed to find out who was supplying the drugs and stop that flow. They decided their best bet was to pay an informant to infiltrate the new drug ring. They chose a woman, known by the pseudonym of Deborah

Downes, who they knew as a drug pusher for the old Black Mafia regime.

Downes did her job, returned to the agents, and told them what she had learned. The word on the street was that the heroin was coming from California. The heroin was being delivered to a drug ring run by a 26-year-old man named Aaron Gant. Once in Kansas City the drugs were cut and doled out to a small army of pushers. The heroin was put into blue capsules that sold for $10 apiece on the streets.

The agents, as well as local police, were already familiar with Gant. He'd been wounded by a shotgun blast in 1972, and was arrested and charged with first-degree murder the following year. The victim in that case had been strangled and was found with hands and feet bound together with electrical cord. Gant was released, however, when the primary witness in that case, who happened to be Gant's ex-girlfriend, decided that she hadn't really seen what she'd told police she'd seen after all.

The agents sent Downes back undercover to set herself up as a drug dealer for the new heroin ring. She attempted to do this but was turned down because Gant and his associates didn't trust her. This temporarily stalled the investigation.

The DEA agents next turned to surveillance, or spying. DEA agents began to follow Gant wherever he went in hopes they could gain some intelligence that might lead to Gant's arrest and successful prosecution. After a time, however, Gant apparently realized that he was being watched. As they followed him one day, the agents saw him throw an envelope out the front window of his black Lincoln Continental. When the agents examined the envelope, it was found to contain a small quantity of marijuana. Gant was arrested and his car was seized. Because the amount of drugs found was so small, the charges of drug possession were dismissed and Gant was released. His car was not. Police sold it at auction. There is a law that allows police to take away a criminal's possessions if those possessions were used when the criminal committed the crime.

The agents needed a new informant who could get inside the heroin operation. A drug user facing possession charges known by the pseudonym Branch Calhoun volunteered for the job. He hoped to avoid jail time by doing a job for the police. He was to infiltrate the drug ring in exchange for having the drug possession charges against him dismissed. Calhoun was told to arrange for purchases

☿ DRUG FORFEITURE LAWS

In the mid-1980s the United States federal government and many state governments passed drug forfeiture laws. These laws allowed the government to seize property from its owner if it could be shown that the property had been used to produce or distribute illegal drugs. The owner of the property does not have to be compensated in any way for the seized property.[1]

Though the Drug Forfeiture Laws have been used as a major weapon in the War on Drugs, they remain controversial. Many people feel that the government uses the laws too frequently, seizing property even when evidence of illegal drug activity is skimpy. Still, the law has been an effective deterrent to possible future drug dealers. According to the U.S. Justice Department, more than $4 billion worth of cars, cash, airplanes, and other property were seized in civil and criminal forfeitures in the first decade of the law's existence.[2]

that would be made under the close surveillance of DEA agents. Because he had not done business with Gant in the past the operation had to proceed slowly. Calhoun began by making small drug purchases from Gant's underlings. He asked a pusher where the drugs were coming from and was told the state of origin was California. The pusher asked Calhoun if he knew any way to get empty capsules, which the ring could fill with the heroin. The drug store that had been their previous source of capsules had been closed down by federal agents. Calhoun said he would check. He reported this back to the agents and was told that getting the capsules would be no problem. In fact, the agents planned to color-code the capsules so they could trace the flow of heroin and see who was handling it. Calhoun supplied the capsules but they were not used. Gant said that they were the wrong size. He had decided from then on that he wanted to sell $15 caps, not $10 caps, so the caps supplied by the agents were obsolete.

Yet another informant was needed. Stan Coffman (a pseudonym), who had recently been arrested for heroin possession while on parole, was eager to make a deal to avoid further prison time. Coffman told the agents that he knew Gant to be the "main man" in the heroin ring. Coffman was assigned to get inside Gant's drug ring and sell heroin for him.

In the meantime a corpse was found strangled with feet and hands bound together with electrical cord. That was Gant's M.O. (method of operation). Coffman told agents that the victim had been murdered because of a drug dispute and that Gant was the murderer. Gant and others were arrested on suspicion but were released on only $35,000 bond apiece.

The drug operation went on, but agents caught a break during the summer of 1976 when a DEA informant purchased heroin from a man named Curtis Jones, who was arrested and agreed to cooperate with the investigation. By that autumn a federal grand jury was convened. A grand jury is made up of citizens (much like a trial jury) who are sworn in by a court to listen to evidence and decide if someone should be charged with a crime. DEA agents and their informants were witnesses. The proceedings only lasted a few days when Gant and others were indicted for (that is, they were formally charged with) distributing heroin in and around Kansas City.

Local police received a tip that Gant, who was still free on bond, was hiding in his mother's home. Police searched the dwelling and Gant surrendered. At trial, with Gant and others as the defendants, prosecutors told a jury that Gant was the head of a heroin ring that made up to $2 million a year. A jury found Gant and all of his co-defendants guilty of drug distribution. They were each sentenced to 13 years in prison, effectively ending Gant's drug ring.

And, for a time, it was much harder to buy heroin in Kansas City.[3]

THE GEORGIA SUPER-METH BUST

Another case that used an informant/surveillance combination to make a big bust began when police in Georgia arrested a small-time dealer in possession of more meth than one addict would use, thus indicating that he was a dealer. Police said that if he supplied some information they would prosecute him as a user rather than a dealer, thereby reducing the seriousness of the charges he faced. The arrested man gave up a few names. Police then called in the DEA.[4]

DEA agents investigated the people named by the informant and put those individuals under surveillance. The residence of one of the suspects proved itself worthy of special attention because of the suspicious number of people who came and went there. So many people were going into and coming out of the residence that it seemed to the agents more like a place of business than a private home. In fact, the residence was "being used in a manner consistent with that of a clandestine methamphetamine laboratory."[5]

In January 2005 a task force made up of DEA agents and several local law enforcement agencies learned that suspects in the case had "purchased large amounts of Drano and muriatic acid on three separate occasions at the ACE Hardware store in Smyrna, Georgia. Drano and muriatic acid are common ingredients used in secret labs to make methamphetamine. The agents also learned that strong chemical smells came from the house."[6]

Close-up view of methamphetamine. *Drug Enforcement Administration*

On February 9, while agents were watching the house, two males exited the rear of the residence and poured a liquid from what appeared to be a trashcan into the yard. Agents later stopped the two men as they left the lab and found about one pound of "ice" (methamphetamine) in their car. The house was searched next and an additional 50 pounds of meth was seized. Investigators learned that the lab had not been used to make meth, but rather to convert regular meth into a stronger and more addictive super-meth.[7]

Special agent in charge Sherri Strange said:

> We have witnessed a rapid evolution of methamphetamine trafficking in the state of Georgia. In just a few years, Georgia has progressed from a spiked increase of ounce-producing 'Mom and Pop' labs, to the importation of hundred-pound quantities of Mexican methamphetamine and ice, to the mass production of meth and ice in 'super-labs' in our own suburban neighborhoods. 'Super-labs' capable of producing ten pounds or more per 'cook,' per day, are virtually unheard of on the East Coast. But drug trafficking like any business operates on a supply and demand basis. As long as the market and demand exist, someone will always be willing to satisfy the need . . . Ice is crack times ten. We must educate the public, the parents, and our youth about methamphetamine and ice and reduce the user population.[8]

THE LAND ROUTE

Many illegal drugs enter the United States by airplane and boat, but large quantities also come in by land. The United States has thousands of miles of land borders with Canada and Mexico, offering a countless number of possible locations through which to smuggle drugs. One successful anti-drug option spanned thousands of miles but still worked like clockwork.

The DEA agents called it Operation Three Hour Tour, borrowing a phrase from the *Gilligan's Island* theme song. A sting is an elaborate setup police use to catch criminals committing a crime, and for 10 months during 2004–2005 the sting had been put in place. The traps had been laid. Three entire drug transportation rings had been found based on tips to the police. The DEA had undercover agents up and down the transportation routes, all the way from Colombia, where the drugs were produced, to major U.S. cities, where the rings had set up their distribution centers. The drug dealers discovered none of the infiltration. In places where infiltration was impossible, DEA agents set up surveillance. The criminals at these locations were being listened to and watched at all times, but they didn't know it. They went about their criminal business while the U.S. anti-drug squad observed them. The rings moved their drugs over the land along a trail that ran through Colombia and Mexico on its way to the United States. Each month the three Mexican and Colombian drug transportation organizations and their U.S. counterparts smuggled and distributed 4,000 pounds of cocaine, 20 to 30 pounds of heroin, and more than 50 pounds of methamphetamine.[9]

During August 2005 the DEA decided that it had accumulated enough evidence against the members of the transportation rings and made 160 arrests. The arrests took place across a wide geographical area: Los Angeles; New York; New Haven, Connecticut; Des Moines, Iowa; the Dominican Republic; and Colombia. All of the arrests were made within three hours of one another. This allowed the agents to work without worrying that one end of the transportation ring had warned the other end that trouble was on its way. The officers seized enough methamphetamine to dry up the supply of 22,700 American addicts. They confiscated 10,000 doses of Ecstasy, 58 vehicles, 216 pounds of marijuana, and $5.5 million in cash. Also seized were 52 firearms, including a .50-caliber assault rifle with armor piercing ammunition, that could have been used in other crimes.[10]

Drug-Sniffing Dogs

In some cases the drug smuggler's worst enemy isn't even human, it's canine. No matter how well-hidden drugs may be, a trained dog can sniff them out with its superior nose. The successful searches made by drug-sniffing dogs have been amazing. Dogs have turned into one of man's most successful anti-drug tools.

STOP AND SMELL THE ... FLOWERS?

In September 1996 Jasper, a trained Springer Spaniel, was brought in to sniff cargo entering England at London's Heathrow Airport. Jasper sniffed out 397 pounds of cocaine hidden in a cargo of flowers aboard a jumbo jet. The drugs had been packed with the flowers in an attempt to mask the aroma. It didn't work. The dog could smell the drugs right through the flowers' strong smell.

In the Tampa Bay area of Florida three years later, sheriff's deputies used a drug-sniffing dog as part of their crackdown on traffic violations. When they stopped a car for swerving on the road, speeding, or running a red light, the deputies brought out Razor, one of their drug-sniffing dogs. Razor was one of a kennel of 10 drug-sniffing dogs employed by that particular sheriff's department. On the average, the dogs were used five times a day to determine if a suspect was in the possession of illegal drugs.

Razor gave each stopped car a sniff. On this day, during the spring of 1999, the police struck pay dirt. After sniffing one car Razor gave the alert signal that he smelled drugs. The deputies considered this reasonable cause to believe there actually were drugs in the car. They performed a search and found morphine and methamphetamine in the vehicle. The driver was arrested and charged with

A drug-sniffing dog works with a canine officer. *Gail Porter/National Institute of Standards and Technology*

drug violations. The driver later sued the sheriff's department for illegally searching his car, claiming that the dog's alert did not give the deputies the right to search his car.

The law says that before police can search a person, his car, or his home, there has to be probable cause. That means there is a reason to believe a crime has been committed. If a woman is heard screaming inside a house, police do not need a search warrant to go inside and look around. If the smell of marijuana is coming from a car, no warrant is needed to search the car.

In 2003 the case made it all the way to the Supreme Court, which decided in favor of the dog and the deputies.[1]

PATIENCE IS A VIRTUE

Sometimes a case begins when police receive an anonymous tip, that is, a phone call from an informant who won't leave his name. In one such instance in 2001, the informer told police that a shipment of drugs was going to arrive the next day at a home in Bel Air, Maryland. When the package was located at an Air Express storage facility, the Narcotics Task Force of the Allegany County Combined Criminal Investigations Unit let their dog, 19-month-old Ladd, get a sniff. The dog—a recent addition to the task force, purchased through community donations—signaled that there were drugs in the package. The police did not make a bust then and there, however. They pretended Ladd had not noticed the drugs and allowed the package to be delivered. They stopped the drug dealers while they were driving. The police wound up seizing 11 pounds of marijuana. The men were charged with possession of marijuana, possession of marijuana with intent to distribute, and possession of marijuana with intent to distribute within a school zone.[2]

According to Wayne Booth of NarcoticDogs.com, who trains what he calls "Narcotic Detector Dogs," the dogs are hand-selected for their temperament and represent only the cream of the crop. They are the exceptionally driven dogs that can work long hours without complaint. The dogs are trained to sniff out marijuana, hashish, cocaine and crack, heroin, and methamphetamine. The truth is that dogs can be trained to sniff out anything that has an odor. If a new drug appeared tomorrow, using chemicals that had never been used to make drugs before, it would only take a few weeks to train a dog to search for the new drug.

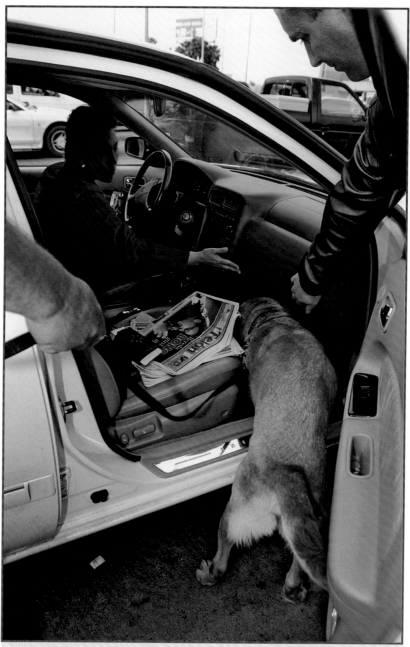

This February 2003 photo shows Spenser, a drug-sniffing yellow Lab, sniffing out methamphetamine hidden in the panels of a car entering the United States from Mexico. *David McNew/Getty Images*

Dogs are trained to search for and detect narcotic odors within vehicles (exterior, interior), luggage/baggage, warehouses, buildings/homes, open areas, and schools. The types of dogs used are Labrador Retrievers, Golden Retrievers, German Shorthair Pointers, German Shepherds, and Belgian Malinois. These breeds are chosen because they instinctively track by scent and have keen senses of smell.

TRAINING THE DOGS

There is a long-standing rumor that dogs are trained to sniff out drugs by first getting the dog addicted to drugs, but this is absolutely untrue. Bill Heiser is an investigator and narcotic K-9 handler with the Volusia County (Florida) sheriff's office and is a United States Police Canine Association National Certified Detector Trainer. He is also the president of Southern Hills Kennels in New Smyrna Beach, Florida, where Bomb and Drug Detection Dogs are trained. The key to training drug-sniffing dogs is to identify the specific smell of various drugs, and to teach the dog to tell the difference between actual drugs and other substances with a similar aroma.[3]

Once the dog learns to tell the difference between the smell of drugs and all other smells, the dog learns how to search places where drugs are most apt to be hidden. Tiny sets are used at some training kennels. There may be a row of school lockers, motor vehicles, a fake airport, or a bus terminal site. Only the dogs that perform best on their final exams are actually used in the field.

Because drug smugglers are clever, and often attempt to fool drug-sniffing dogs by placing drugs inside or with other highly aromatic substances, the dogs are trained to find drugs even when the scent is camouflaged. Some of the odors used to camouflage the smell of drugs include food, talcum powder, perfume, mothballs, deodorants, gasoline, and flowers.

Dogs must learn to find the drugs without biting or grabbing them, since this could cause the dog to accidentally ingest the drugs. Dogs signal that they have found drugs by showing an excited demeanor. Dogs can be trained to detect more than one kind of drug. For example, a dog already trained to find marijuana could subsequently be trained to find cocaine. However, once a dog has been trained as a drug-sniffer, it can no longer be used for any other kind of work.

The training techniques combine two things that come naturally to dogs. They hunt with their noses, and they want to please their handlers. When a dog is ready to go into the field, it is matched up with a human handler. Another two weeks of training transform the dog and handler into a team ready to fight crime.

Before becoming a drug-sniffing dog for the U.S. Customs Service, a dog must complete a 12-week course. Dogs that graduate and are assigned to duty are those who score perfectly in their final exam. The dogs must be able to tell the difference between a package that contains drugs from one that does not 100 percent of the time. The dogs are taught to tell the difference between a "live" scent and a "dead" scent. That is, they can distinguish between a package that contains drugs and one that used to contain drugs but no longer does.[4]

There are two types of drug-sniffing dogs. *Proactive* dogs (Labradors, retrievers, and spaniels) sniff baggage, aircraft holds, freight sheds, vehicles, ships, and homes. *Passive* dogs sniff drugs hidden on people. They sit next to the drug couriers and wag their tails.

Bill Heiser trains some of his dogs to sniff out drugs, others to sniff out explosives. During the 1990s Heiser used to sell 20 drug-sniffers for every bomb-sniffer. Today those numbers are reversed. Since the attacks of September 11, 2001, homeland security uses personnel, both human and canine, that used to be on the frontlines of the War on Drugs.

MATCHING DOG AND HANDLER

The training of the dog is completed before the dog and its new police officer partner meet. The easy part is over. Training the dog is almost always easier than training the human. Just as drug-sniffing dogs must pass through a screening process, so too must the handlers. Just as specific breeds of dog are best for drug-sniffing, certain types of people make the best handlers. All handlers are carefully screened to eliminate those who might be incompatible with the dog. Handlers must take a written test and earn a certificate before they become eligible to handle a drug-sniffing dog. Once the handler and dog are joined there is a second training period, during which the handler learns how to use the dog to find drugs, and the handler and dog bond.

The pair becomes an inseparable team after that. Police come from far away to the small number of dog-training facilities in the United States. Training is just as demanding on the human as it is on the dog. Not everyone passes the rigorous, three-week training course. Those that fail are sent home without a dog. Only the very best officers pass and are allowed to team up with a dog in the field.[5]

For the human trainees the course begins with a few hours of lectures. Heiser tells the humans that they will be "sleeping, eating, and breathing with their dog." After the trainer prepares the new students, the humans are led into a large warehouse, each holding a leash. The dogs are then allowed in, and the dogs decide which human they want to work with. The dogs will sniff around the humans for a while and stay near the one they are most comfortable with.

The dog/human team is then subjected to a series of lessons and tests. The humans learn the commands the dogs have been trained to respond to in order to get the dog to perform its duty. They also learn the proper procedures for a wide variety of circumstances. For

♀ DOGS AND YOUR RIGHTS

Does the use of drug-sniffing dogs violate one's constitutional rights? Does having a dog sniff a person's luggage violate his or her rights against unreasonable search and seizure? Authorities need a court order signed by a judge in order to search someone's home without permission from the owner. The standard is that if there is a "reasonable cause" to believe a crime has been committed, then the judge will sign the search warrant. But the Supreme Court says that a dog alert outside a home is not enough reasonable cause for the inside of the home to be searched.

The Supreme Court ruled, however, that it is legal for police to use drug-sniffing dogs to help search cars if there is a reasonable cause to believe drugs are being transported, such as might be the case if the car was swerving. Such was the case in the Florida bust that resulted from Razor's keen senses detecting drugs in a stopped car.[6]

example, when a dog is sniffing a room, the human should lead it along every wall and into all four corners. The human should make sure the dog is getting its nose right down to the seams where the floor meets the wall. When the dogs perform a task correctly, their human rewards them. The dog gets to play fetch with a tennis ball, which is a drug-sniffing dog's favorite all-time activity, or it gets a belly rub while the human says things like, "That's a good boy! That's such a good boy! Atta boy!" Playing tug of war with a favorite toy is also a favorite game. Even though the dogs have a very serious role, they are as happy and playful as other dogs.

During the final exam in Heiser's program the dog and his partner must find drugs planted in different places. The final test involves three parked cars. The human/canine teams must search each vehicle and figure out which of the cars has cocaine hidden behind its right headlight.

Wiretaps and Other Types of Electronic Surveillance

On April 7, 2005, Australian police used wiretaps to break a huge Ecstasy ring. Wiretaps are listening devices that allow authorities to hear other people's phone conversations without their presence being known. When working with wiretaps, police usually like to put off the actual bust for as long as possible, as long as no one is being hurt and the suspects are still talking. Convicting criminals and getting maximum prison sentences calls for as much evidence as possible. But on this day, the police heard the drug ring's leaders having this conversation:

Man #1:"You know that thing today? Is it finished?"

Man #2: "Not yet."

Man #1: "You better work out what you're doing because they're onto us."

Those words put the police into action. In this case, *police* means a joint force of investigators from the Australian Federal Police (much like the U.S. FBI), customs, and the Australian Crime Commission.

Once suspects know they are being spied upon, the bust must be made. Raids on two houses in the Australian city of Melbourne followed. Police seized a total of 5 million Ecstasy tablets, with an estimated street value of $250 million. Four persons were arrested at two locations.

A private investigator demonstrates how to use a phone-tapping device in Rome, Italy, in October 2006. *Chris Warde-Jones/Bloomberg News/Landov*

The bust was one of the largest ever, anywhere in the world, and police had electronic technology to thank for it. It was their ability to legally listen in on the phone conversations of suspected criminals that allowed the bust to happen.

The two men on the tape, along with two other men at the second location, were arrested. The investigative team had known whose phones to tap after receiving a tip about a suspicious shipping container filled with ceramic tiles bound for Melbourne from Italy. When the container arrived at the Australian dock, an X-ray was taken and revealed that there were millions of pellet-sized objects in the container. Police tapped the phones of the people who were scheduled to pick up the crate. The drugs were removed from the crate and replaced by fake pills. When the criminals came to pick up the crate the police followed them as they drove to a factory and two of the arrests were made.[1]

COURT ORDERS

Sophisticated surveillance devices are powerful tools to capture criminals. But the usage of the surveillance equipment must not be abused. It would be wrong, for example, for a public official to use the technology to spy on his enemies or to use it to gather information that could be useful in defeating his political opponents. It is for those reasons that all wiretaps and other surveillance may only be done legally with permission from a judge. This permission is called a warrant. It indicates that a judge feels the surveillance is justified by the situation. It is the same type of warrant that law enforcement agents must get before searching a person's home without their permission. The standard for granting a warrant is that there must be a reasonable cause to believe a crime is being committed before the phone tap and other surveillance equipment can be legally used.

? WEARING A WIRE

Throughout the War on Drugs, a popular method of gathering evidence against drug traffickers is to get an informant, or a mole, to wear a wire. That is, they hide a microphone on their person somewhere and record everything that happens around them, including a criminal either committing crimes or admitting to committing crimes. Today these listening devices are so small that they are nearly impossible to detect, but this was not always the case. The first wires, worn in the early 1970s, were packs a little bit larger than a deck of cards that fit onto a person's belt. They were bulky, could be found during a routine frisking or pat down, and were never guaranteed to work properly.

STATE OF THE ART EQUIPMENT

After getting a court order, police can use different types of electronic surveillance to catch criminals and break up drug-trafficking rings. Today, more than ever, the equipment used allows agents to see and hear what the criminals are doing with little chance that the criminals will soon figure out that they are being spied upon. For example, police have cameras that fit onto a button. An undercover agent can make a drug buy, stand face to face with a drug dealer, and capture the entire buy on video. And the criminal is never the wiser.

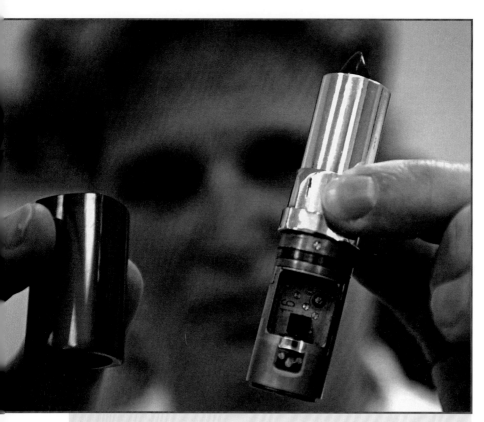

A woman holds up a tube of lipstick that contains a hidden camera similar to the ones sometimes used in drug investigations. *Peter Forster/dpa/Landov*

Many people have a cell phone with a built-in camera, but law enforcement agents have special cell phones with the camera built into the side. That way, the agent can take a photo of the criminal while holding the phone to his ear as if talking on the phone. No one can tell that a photo is being taken.

Other common hiding places for video cameras are in the frames of eyeglasses, in a woman's lipstick, or a belt buckle. Rooms can be videotaped with a camera hidden inside a piece of furniture. Criminals often never know that there is a camera on them and a microphone capturing their every move and word. They often don't find out until they are forced to watch and hear themselves in a court of law.[2]

Because the spying equipment used by cops has grown so sophisticated, video and audio surveillance is far more common-place today than it was 30 years ago. The DEA was ahead of its time when it came to using camera equipment to create evidence that would stand up in court against drug smugglers and drug dealers. The cameras and the microphones used 30 years ago were much larger, so it was more difficult to use them in secret. On the other hand, way back in the day, people weren't as apt to look for them either.

Today, when just about everyone uses a cell phone, it is simple to determine who is talking to whom and for how long. Cell phone records keep track of the phone numbers that are dialed on that phone and how long each conversation lasts. Before cell phones, only long-distance phone conversations could be tracked. Back then, police would put a device on a criminal's phone called the pen register, or dialed number recorder. Attached to a phone it would record the pulses made by the dialing of the phone and allow investigators to figure out the phone numbers their subject was calling. In order to legally attach a pen register to a subject's phone a court order was necessary, just as is the case with wiretaps and other electronic surveillance devices.

Difficulty in Busting Drug Barons

Next to the illegal arms industry, the drug trade is the largest illegal industry in the world. It was estimated in 2005 by the United Nations Office on Drugs and Crime that more than $300 billion are spent worldwide on drugs each year. The profits from all of that business end up in the pockets of a small number of people: the world's drug barons. Although some drug barons live in well-developed nations such as the United States and the United Kingdom, they wield the most power in smaller, underdeveloped nations such as Thailand, Afghanistan, and Bolivia, where the drug trade provides a large percentage of the national economy.

Some of these small countries' economies are dependent on the drug trade. Many of their people depend on the drug trade to earn money for the food they eat and the shelter over their heads. Colombia, for example, earns a half billion dollars a year in drug profits.[1] Although the leaders of these drug-dependent countries may say out loud that they are eager to wipe out the drug trade in their nation, they also realize that, without the production and export of illegal drugs, their countries would be much poorer than they are today. This is true despite the fact that the great majority of the money ends up in only a handful of pockets.[2]

Because of their enormous wealth, the barons are among the most powerful people in the world. In some cases they control the government of their home country. They have bribed politicians and judges so they can operate unhindered by law enforcement. A United Nations conference called the Vienna Convention (VC) can pass laws that are then recognized by nations that belong to the U.N. The VC has passed laws that allow police to freeze the assets of drug barons. Before the assets can be frozen, however, it must be shown that the money was made through illegal drug trade. Since it can be difficult to prove how drug barons make their money, the VC's laws have seldom proved successful. It is difficult to trace any of the barons' possessions or cash to drug crimes because of sophisticated money-laundering techniques. **Money laundering** is taking money earned from committing a crime and investing it, spending it, or processing it in such a way that the criminal no longer has in his possession cash that might connect him to the crime. Some drug-trafficking rings have been broken up not because they were caught dealing in drugs, but because they were caught illegally laundering their money. Barons often keep their money in secure bank accounts and locally, where police from other countries are no match for the local police who have been paid well to protect the drug baron.

No one in the drug baron's community wants the police from another nation to arrest the baron. The baron often employs many people in his region. Farmers grow the plants from which drugs are derived. Workers run plants to change the raw materials into usable drugs. Packagers and shippers help move the drugs. They all work for the drug baron.

It can be a dangerous business going after a drug baron. Take, for example, the case of New York journalist Manuel de Dios Unanue. He liked to investigate and report on tough subjects, and during the 1980s and early 1990s he wrote a series of articles for the Spanish-language newspaper *El Diario-La Prensa* about the methods of one baron's "Cali Cartel." Soon thereafter, in March of 1992, he was shot dead inside a New York City restaurant. His killer was captured and convicted in 1994, and it was revealed during his trial that Unanue's killing had been ordered by Colombia drug baron José Santacruz Londono.[3]

Another difficulty in attacking the drug barons in other countries is that U.S. agents often meet resistance from the highest levels of foreign governments. In August 2005, for example, Venezuelan President Hugo Chavez accused the DEA of using its agents to spy on him and his government rather than working to stop the illegal drug trade. Because of this alleged espionage, he refused to cooperate in any way with the DEA agents in Venezuela. Chavez

Colombian peasant Wilmar Ospina, a coca grower, checks one of his coca plants in May 2001. A large portion of Colombia's economy depends on the drug trade. *Reuters/Corbis*

publicly stated that "the DEA isn't absolutely necessary for the fight against drug trafficking." He said that the United States was being hypocritical when it came to battling illegal drugs. The country, Chavez said, was the world's largest consumer of drugs and yet they did little to reduce the number of drug users inside America. He claimed that, although DEA and FBI agents pursued drug barons in Venezuela, they ignored the drug barons who were living inside the United States. Criticisms of Chavez's words were few from official sources in the United States, although officials hoped to maintain a productive relationship in the fight against drugs.[4]

FUNDING THE BATTLE OVERSEAS

In the days before September 11, 2001, the United States pumped hundreds of millions of dollars into funding the war on drugs overseas. For example, in 2000 the United States spent close to a billion dollars on combating the production and export of cocaine and marijuana in Colombia.[5]

One of the production areas busted in Colombia that year was a shack in the northern section of the country where green coca leaves were crushed and processed with chemicals such as acetone and ammonia into a golden colored paste. This is the first step in converting the leaves into cocaine. In the past such operations might have gone unhindered, but with the United States funding police efforts in that area, authorities busted the shack and put it out of business. The shack was burned, just as more than 150 others running similar operations in that region were burned that year. But the businesses were not put out of operation forever. The disruption in the production of coca paste was probably minor when looking at the big picture. With drug baron money behind them, the shacks and the processing plants were rebuilt and back in operation in a matter of weeks, in new locations. General Ismael Trujillo, chief of Colombia's anti-narcotics police, was asked by a reporter if he felt frustrated that he could only slow the production of cocaine a little bit, despite all of his efforts. He said that the drug trade needed to be battled. "Are we supposed to just cross our arms?" he asked. "We have to draw the line somewhere. This has to be a permanent battle. Otherwise the world will pay the consequences."[6]

Even before the terrorist attacks of 2001 changed U.S. priorities, there was debate about the wisdom of spending so much money in Colombia battling drugs. It was a good cause, but how could authorities make sure the money was being spent the way the United States had intended. There was always a chance that the drug busts reported to U.S. officials were token in nature, meant only to appease the United States. There was a chance that all of that money was doing more harm than good, that a good chunk of it was ending up in the pockets of the drug barons themselves.[7]

Today the United States still sends money to the anti-drug forces of Colombia, but not as much as before homeland security became America's top priority.

OPERATION HABITAT

In one case men very close to the top of a drug cartel were caught and arrested. They were successfully prosecuted and are currently serving long prison terms in Great Britain. Here's how it happened.

Using an intelligence operation that lasted more than four years, a billion dollar drug-smuggling ring was smashed in the first weeks of 2006 in Great Britain. The successful operation was undertaken by a team of agencies, in this case local British police departments, Scotland Yard, Britain's National Crime Squad, and Colombian authorities.

The operation started in 2001, a full four and a half years before its successful conclusion. More than 60 arrests resulted, but the big news was the quantity of drugs the ring had smuggled into Great Britain, an estimated 20 tons of drugs worth about £1 billion. The smuggling ring employed an army of couriers and money launderers to smuggle shipments past customs officials and return the proceeds to South America.

Law enforcement finally caught up with the **cartel** through its money-laundering operations, the portion of the investigation conducted by Scotland Yard. The case broke when Scotland Yard learned that a café and a travel agency in the northern section of London were two of the businesses being used to launder the cartel's money. The initial raids allowed police to seize £3.5 million and almost 650 kilograms of cocaine.[8]

Although not too many details about the investigation were revealed, the National Crime Squad did say that two years' worth of "intrusive surveillance techniques" were used to gather evidence. It was unknown if this meant a mole was in place, if electronic surveillance devices were used, or possibly a combination of the two.[9]

The men running the cartel were Jesus Anibal Ruiz-Henao, 45, and his brother-in-law, Mario Tascon, 32. The men came to Britain

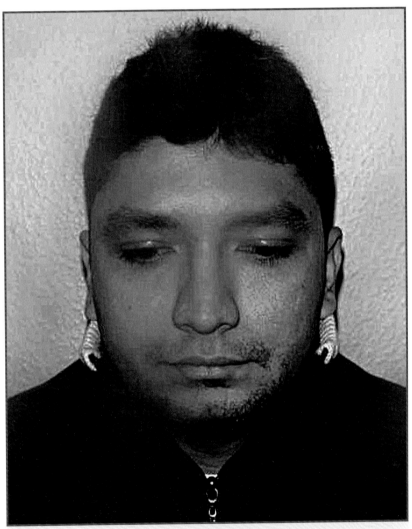

Mario Tascon, who was sentenced to 17 years in prison in the United Kingdom for supplying class A drugs, is shown in this police picture released on January 6, 2006. *Reuters/Landov*

in 1990. They claimed they were seeking asylum from persecution in their home country of Colombia. British authorities bought the story and allowed them to stay in Britain "indefinitely." They took jobs as a bus driver and a cleaner, but these were only covers

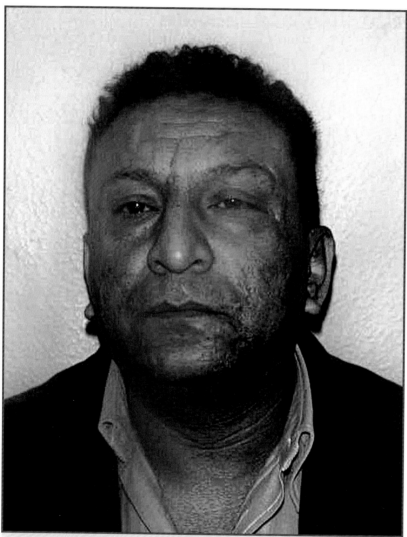

Jesus Anibal Ruiz-Henao was sentenced to 19 years in prison for his role in a gang that ran the biggest cocaine and money-laundering operation ever to be uncovered in the United Kingdom. *Reuters/ Landov*

for their real activities. The men immediately began to set up business, smuggling drugs from Colombia into Great Britain. By the time they were arrested more than a decade later, they were making tens of millions of British pounds a year, and not much of it came from cleaning and driving a bus. Perhaps to help explain the amount of cash he had, Ruiz-Henao became the director of a charity to help orphans in London. Ruiz-Henao and Tascon were responsible for such a large portion of the cocaine brought into Great Britain every year that, when authorities put them out of business, the price of cocaine in that country rose 20 percent due to short supply.

According to Detective Superintendent Martin Molloy of the National Crime Squad, this was the largest drug cartel ever smashed by British law enforcement. He called it the "first billion-pound drugs cartel that we have ever dealt with."[10]

The judge at the trial, Judge Nicholas Loraine-Smith, explained to the Scottish newspaper, *The Scotsman*, that it was rare that men this high in a cartel get busted. Loraine-Smith said,

> This is because they pay other people to carry out the danger-ous work where an arrest is more likely. Their fingerprints are not found on the drug packaging, no telephone is shown to have made relevant calls, nothing incriminating is found in their homes. Others carry out their tasks. Meanwhile, they make enormous profits from this foul trade.[11]

According to Detective Sergeant Ian Floyd of Scotland Yard, the cartel smuggled its drugs in a variety of ways, often by couriers or packed in pallets in the back of trucks and covered in mustard to disguise the smell from sniffer dogs. They were also hidden in fruit or dissolved into liquid form and ingrained into clothing or plastic. The cocaine was usually taken from Colombia via ship to the coast of Spain or Portugal, where smaller craft would smuggle it ashore. Trucks would then transport it to Britain. Once in this country, it was split into parcels and taken to safe houses around the country, from where it was sent to local distributors and eventually to street dealers.[12]

As there are drug mules to carry drugs past customs, there are also money mules who smuggle the money earned from drug sales back to the country where the drugs originated. One money mule

° PUNISHING THE GUILTY

Another way to fight the War on Drugs is to make sure that drug criminals convicted in court spend a long time in prison. Both state and federal laws in the United States have been updated throughout the years to keep up with the growing drug problem. Strong anti-drug laws work in two ways. They keep convicted drug criminals out of business for long stretches of time, and they show possible future drug criminals that it is wise to go into another line of work. The U.S. federal government has been using conspiracy and money-laundering laws, called RICO Laws, to combat drugs. RICO stands for the Racketeer Influenced and Corrupt Organizations Act. Congress passed the set of laws in the fall of 1970. It allowed law enforcement to arrest mobsters who were part of a conspiracy to commit a crime. Anyone who was part of an organization that was committing a crime and helped that organization commit the crime, was guilty of committing the crime, whether or not they actually pulled the trigger or robbed the bank. The crime was called racketeering, which meant conspiring with others to profit from an illegal business of some sort. The laws, while originally passed to fight organized crime, now also put drug traffickers in prison. Leaders of drug gangs and their lieutenants can be put away for 30-plus years. Using the RICO Laws, the murders committed by drug gangs are used as evidence of the criminal conspiracy and not as crimes in and of themselves.[13]

busted in this case had condoms stuffed with 100 Euro notes in his stomach.[14]

Ruiz-Henao and Tascon are currently serving sentences of 19 and 17 years, respectively, and additional sentences of 10 and 9 years for money laundering.

The Flow
of Drugs

Until the early 1970s heroin arrived in the United States through what was known as the French Connection. Poppies were grown in the fields of Turkey. The poppies were converted into raw opium then transported through Syria and Lebanon to the Mediterranean Sea. From the cities of the Middle East the opium was moved by land and sea to cities in Europe. There, in large processing plants, the opium was converted into heroin.

The largest of all of these heroin-processing plants was in the city of Marseilles, France. The plant was operated by French organized crime. Not only was the most heroin produced in Marseilles, the highest-quality heroin was produced there as well. The finished heroin was formed into bricks and smuggled into the United States.

The award-winning movie *The French Connection* (1971), showed how law enforcement prevented one shipment of heroin from getting to drug dealers in the United States. In the movie, which was based on an actual bust, 150 pounds of heroin was hidden inside a high-end automobile owned by a French television star. Police confiscated the heroin and busted several American members of organized crime who were on the receiving end of the drug shipment.

The real French Connection was finally broken up in the 1970s when the United States pressured Turkey to stop the illegal planting and harvesting of poppies. Turkey still grows poppies but most of them are for the legal production of opiate drugs, such as codeine, that one might be prescribed after minor surgery.[1]

THE GOLDEN TRIANGLE

With Turkey's illegal poppy-growing business squashed, other countries picked up the slack. Poppy plants began to come from the Southeast Asian countries of Burma, Laos, and Thailand, known as the Golden Triangle. The poppies are processed into opium inside these countries and then moved to the coastal regions. Some of the drugs are smuggled into the United States by way of Hong Kong and Singapore. Other shipments go through European cities on their way to North America.[2]

A woman harvests opium poppies in Burma. The supply of poppy plants from Burma, Laos, and Thailand is known as the Golden Triangle.
Christophe Loviny/Corbis

In the Golden Triangle the drug barons who own the land are so rich that they have their own armies to protect their crops and their number-one export: opium. The forces protecting the drug operation are stronger than any forces trying to stop them. Although the drug barons have been known to fight one another, outside forces have been able to do little to stop the production of opium in these three countries.

In the 1980s the Thai government tried to attack the drug barons. Resistance was stiff, and when the attacks were successful the barons simply crossed the border into Burma and set up new operations. When the government attacks subsided, the drug barons returned to Thailand.

THE GOLDEN CRESCENT

Another opium-producing area is called the Golden Crescent, consisting of regions in Pakistan, Iran, and Afghanistan. Unlike the French Connection or the Golden Triangle, most of the drugs produced in the Golden Crescent are not exported. Instead they are consumed in those three countries. According to a United Nations report, Iran has the highest rate of drug addiction in the world. The U.N. World Drug Report for 2005 estimated that close to 3 percent of Iranians over the age of 15 were drug addicts.[3]

The drug-trading center of the Golden Crescent is Landi Kotal, located in the western provinces of Pakistan. The opium that is exported from the Golden Crescent travels by land, usually by car or camel, through Turkey and from Turkey to other European countries.[4]

THE PIZZA CONNECTION

The flow of heroin from Italy to the United States took a hit in the 1980s when a task force led by United States Attorney (and later mayor of New York) Rudy Giuliani busted 22 heroin traffickers who had been part of a trafficking route in which heroin entered the United States and was distributed through storefronts disguised as pizza parlors. The case was broken when several drug traffickers were arrested at an airport in Palermo, Italy, for trying to smuggle in the equivalent of millions of dollars in cash. Information gathered

Mafia boss Tommaso Buscetta arrives at the airport in Rome in September 1984 after being extradited from Brazil. Buscetta provided key evidence in the so-called Pizza Connection case. *AP Photo*

from those men helped focus an investigation in the United States conducted jointly by the FBI and the New York Police Department. When a mobster named Tommaso Buscetta was arrested in New York on separate charges, he agreed to give up evidence regarding the pizza parlor scheme in exchange for a lighter sentence. Other mobsters under arrest followed Buscetta's lead and law enforcement eventually had a parade of criminals willing to testify against the so-called Pizza Connection.[5]

The court case took a year and a half and resulted in 18 convictions. Of those arrested, two of the men pleaded guilty, and two others were shot dead by their cohorts to prevent them from turning into informants.[6]

SOUTH OF THE BORDER

Not all heroin-producing poppies are grown on the other side of the world. Some are grown within the borders of Mexico. Because Mexico is so close to the United States, getting the drug from the supplier to the consumer is easier than transporting it from Asia or the Middle East. The Mexican government's anti-drug forces will kill illegal poppy plants when it finds them, but its efforts are often inadequate, and the supply of Mexican heroin into the United States has grown so much that Mexico is now the primary drug corridor into the United States.[7]

Even though much less heroin is produced in Mexico than in the Golden Triangle or Golden Crescent, it is estimated that Mexican heroin makes up a larger portion of the U.S. heroin supply than drugs from the other two regions. It is easy to figure out why this is true. Mexico is much closer to the United States than the other regions and the two countries share many hundreds of miles of unprotected border.[8]

SELF-DEFENDERS

The supply of illegal drugs into the United States from the south is facilitated along the way by revolutionary groups seeking to overthrow their government and independent military groups violently opposed to anything that might slow the flow of drugs. Both groups are financed in large part by drug barons. In Colombia the private group is known as the Self-Defenders. Its purpose is to do whatever it takes to protect its sponsors' interests. The group is so powerful and feared that no drug smuggler can run a successful operation out of Colombia without paying it a fee and becoming a client.

The Self-Defenders' activities over the years have included acts of terrorism, the assassination of top anti-drug agents, and guerilla warfare against law enforcement. When Colombian President Alvaro Uribe was inaugurated in 2002, the ceremony was marred by a mortar attack on the Presidential Palace. The Colombian pro-drug forces do not just work in Colombia. They have spread out to cover the length of the "pipeline" through which cocaine flows into the U.S.[9]

THE TERRORISM/DRUG CONNECTION

The 9/11 attacks caused U.S. national security forces to reprioritize. Since protecting the nation from the inflow of illegal drugs and from terrorism involve overlap in law-enforcement techniques, the same military and police forces tend to protect Americans from both. On the other end, the efforts of terrorist and drug-smuggling groups also overlap. In some cases, they are one and the same. Heroin production in Afghanistan supports the Taliban, the same group that financed Al Qaeda and paid for the 9/11 attacks. As of 2008 U.S. military forces are still in Afghanistan fighting the Taliban and searching for Osama bin Laden, the mastermind of the 9/11 attacks. In the process, the U.S. is fighting a literal war against drugs.[10]

The War
on Drugs Today

Probably the most important single time period in the history of illegal drug use in the United States and the world was the 1960s. During this decade, a large segment of the population came to believe it was okay to take illegal drugs. Before the 1960s the average American may have thought only musicians and teenaged hoodlums took drugs, and drug use was seen as unacceptable by the great majority of Americans.

DRUGS BECOME POPULAR

In the 1960s recreational drug use, taking drugs to get high and not for medicinal purposes, became an accepted part of what was called the hippie lifestyle. Hippies held disdain for the "establishment" and tried to live outside society's moral and monetary framework. The hippy movement was galvanized by its opposition to the Vietnam War, but also embraced a wide variety of liberal ideals such as communal living. For as long as there have been drugs there have been pleasure-seekers, many of whom have become drug addicts, to the detriment of both themselves and their community. In the first half of the twentieth century, recreational drug use was not unheard of, but it was not widespread or done openly. It became a more serious problem for mainstream society when drugs became an accepted norm of a growing counter-culture that consisted mostly of young people, many of whom opposed the Vietnam War (1959–1975).

Hippies, as these young people were commonly known, openly experimented with marijuana and hallucinogenic drugs such as LSD. An LSD experience was called "taking a trip." The drug culture and its psychedelic fashions gained further acceptance when popular rock musicians of the time sang songs about the effects of LSD and other drugs.

People from all walks of life began to experiment with drugs. Knowledge of drug use became so widespread that drug terms like "you're trippin'" and "having the munchies" became recognizable phrases among people who didn't abuse drugs.

Although the use of hallucinogens skyrocketed during the hippie era, the use of opiates, such as heroin, did not. Some hippies distinguished between drugs that were smoked or swallowed and "needle drugs," which they considered to be for losers. By the 1970s the hippie movement had peaked, its relevance diminished by decreased American military involvement in Southeast Asia, but drug usage continued to spread. Pandora's Box had been opened.

With the slackening of social pressures against drug use, the number of Americans who experimented with drugs rose. In 1960 an estimated four million Americans had tried illegal drugs. According to the Drug Enforcement Administration, in 2008 there were about 74 million Americans who had tried illegal drugs at least once in their lifetime.[1]

KEEPING UP TO DATE

Drug enforcement officials stay up to date about how drugs are being sold. There was a time when agents looking for marijuana could assume that they'd either find plants growing in soil or marijuana packed in plastic bags for sale. It usually looked about the same, a combination of leaves, stems, and seeds. That is no longer the case. Today marijuana often doesn't look at all like marijuana.

In October 2005 DEA agents received a tip that a man in suburban Oakland, California, was making something called "Beyond Bomb," which was candy laced with marijuana. The product was designed to be marketed to young consumers. Upon further investigation, DEA agents—working with police in Richmond, Oakland, Lafayette, and two county narcotics enforcement teams—learned

During a 2006 raid of an Oakland, California, marijuana factory, DEA agents seized marijuana packaged to look like candy. *Drug Enforcement Administration*

that the same manufacturer was also making soft drinks with pot mixed in.

The candy and drinks had names such as "Stoney Ranchers," "Rasta Reese's," "Buddahfinger," and "Pot Tarts." The information resulted in four simultaneous raids on warehouses in the Oakland area. In addition to the marijuana-laced candy and soda, agents also found between 4,000 and 5,000 marijuana plants, $100,000 in cash, two semi-automatic weapons, and a revolver.[2]

DRUG HOUSES

Drug houses are houses that are used to produce drugs. They may appear to be normal urban, suburban, or rural homes, but inside they are something else. Sometimes they are small chemistry labs. Sometimes they are greenhouses, used to grow marijuana.

In the small California town of Elm Grove, there was a rash of homes purchased and used to produce drugs by members of Asian gangs that operate out of San Francisco. In 2006 alone, 40 such houses were busted by local law enforcement. The houses cost about a half million dollars each. After each house was purchased the new owners simply pulled the blinds so neighbors couldn't see in, and equipped the place to be an efficient, pot-growing green-house. The drug producers installed special hot lamps and covered the floors with rich soil. The pot-growing systems installed were very sophisticated. According to the Associated Press:

> Walls and ceilings were smashed to allow for complex ventila-
> tion and filtration systems that vented the telltale odor of pot
> through the attic. A web of extension cords and makeshift
> electric panels was used to illegally tap into the outside grid
> to avoid detection and save thousands of dollars in expenses.
> Most of the targeted homes were bought for between $400,000
> and $600,000. Hundreds of thousands of dollars were spent
> to convert each of them to grow millions of dollars worth of
> marijuana.[3]

The gangs purchased the houses because they thought they would be a safe place to operate. Suspicious neighbors reported the first house, and police followed up and busted the marijuana growers there. After that, law enforcement agents made a list of houses purchased in towns east of San Francisco by Chinese men with roots in the big city. Many of these purchases were innocent, but police quickly discovered a pattern of gang members setting up their drug producing facilities out of town.

Up until this time the police had usually looked outside for the marijuana plants. Now, they realized, pot plants might no longer be visible from police helicopters overhead with a roof in the way. Canadian Police had previously found similar drug houses in British Columbia, Canada. Police believed the operation had moved south to San Francisco because of increased border patrols after 9/11. According to Rodney Benson, the DEA's agent in charge of Wash-ington, Oregon, Alaska, and Idaho: "It's definitely a concerted effort by Asian organized crime groups in Canada to move part of their operation down to the United States."[4] Although the busts ham-pered the drug distribution and sales cartel of the Asian gangs, they didn't come close to putting the gangs out of business. Although victory over the cartel may not be around the corner, neither is defeat, and law enforcement in Canada and California continue to fight small battles against drugs in hopes that one day the big battle can be won.

BUSTING AN ECSTASY LAB

Law enforcement agents need to know as much as possible about how a drug is made and distributed. For example, if police know exactly which materials are needed to make a drug such as MDMA (3,4-methylenedioxymethamphetamine, commonly known as Ecstasy), they can monitor the sale and purchase of those materials, and try to expose and stop a drug-making lab before it even begins.[5]

That was the way police in Detroit, Michigan, stopped an Ecstasy ring in 2001. Police there knew exactly which chemicals were needed to make Ecstasy and were monitoring all of the sources for those chemicals.[6] When someone purchased unusual amounts of those chemicals—for example someone purchasing gallons of the essential oil safrole used to make Ecstasy—they received a visit from police. During the autumn of 2001 DEA agents arrested two drug makers in their lab and charged them with "possessing materials necessary to produce Ecstasy"[7] and "possession of equipment to manufacture controlled substances."[8] The lab was located in an apartment in a building mostly occupied by college students. As a bonus, when the lab was raided, police also found marijuana and packaging materials.[9]

Susan Feld, a spokeswoman from the DEA's Detroit office, said:

They had purchased and received equipment to manufacture Ecstasy. They hadn't started making it because they were waiting on the last chemical to be delivered. Several of the chemicals were hazardous and could have done damage to the neighborhood. Those have been removed. They'll probably face charges for some of the chemicals, and the marijuana charges.[10]

The raid took place early in the morning, waking one of the suspects up. He woke to see DEA officials setting up a light fixture shining into the apartment. According to a neighbor who watched the raid: "They had DEA bulletproof vests on and police jackets. Some of them had guns strapped to their upper thighs. At one point there were two or four wearing gas masks."[11]

STALKING DUMPSITES WITH EUROPOL (EUROPEAN POLICE OFFICE)

Europol is the official police agency of the European Union (EU). It gathers intelligence across national borders and helps the EU's member nations in their fight against drug trafficking and other forms of serious organized crime.

Europol's most recent big drug bust came in January 2006. Two chemical labs and two drug warehouses were raided, putting a big dent in the Ecstasy and meth trade in Europe. The raids took place in Belgium, the Netherlands, and Germany, and 21 persons were arrested in all. More than 100,000 gallons of chemicals were seized, as was the equipment necessary to produce Ecstasy and meth.

The investigation that led to the arrests was a little different from most others. Europol agents sought out cases of illegal chemical dumping. They visited these sites and tested each one to see if the chemicals being dumped were the same as those used to make illegal drugs. They found matches in the Netherlands, Germany, and Belgium. They staked out those dumpsites, and the next time chemicals were dumped at those locations, the agents followed the dump vehicle back to its home. In each case they discovered the lab where the drugs were made. After making the busts, police learned that the busted drug rings had been in operation for three years and had produced thousands of pounds of illegal drugs. About the successful raids, the director of Europol, Max-Peter Ratzel, said, "The fight against drug trafficking is and will remain a priority for us."[12]

THE DRUG-IDENTITY THEFT CONNECTION

Some drug crimes don't easily fit into a category. Federal authorities cracked such a case in 2004. A drug-trafficking ring in the Baltimore, Maryland-Washington, D.C.-area, got their victims hooked on cocaine, crack, or heroin, then took out life insurance policies

Ecstasy tablets in a typical Ecstasy lab. This lab was raided by police in Sao Paolo, Brazil, in August 2000. *AP Photo/Dado Galdieri*

in their names and collected when the victims died. Pilfered Social Security numbers and other stolen personal information were used without the victim's knowledge to fill out the insurance paperwork. This information may also be used to steal money from someone's bank account or fraudulently open a credit card, a type of crime called identity theft.[13]

United States Attorney Thomas M. DiBiagio said, "What makes the indictment so unique is this is the first time we've come across a drug organization laundering proceeds in this fashion." In the past, he explained, drug gangs that wanted to maximize profits would set up retail shops such as auto parts stores, buy inventory with the drug proceeds, then double their money through sales, DiBiagio said. Identity theft is apparently just the latest method. "They are businessmen. They realize this is a way to make more money," he said.[14]

Identity theft expert Rob Douglas, who has testified before Congress several times on the topic, said:

> If the allegations contained in the indictment are true, this is the most despicable use of identity theft I have ever encountered. To sell life-threatening drugs to addicts, while collecting the proceeds of fraudulently procured life insurance

♀ DIRTY PIPES

If a drug lab has been abandoned, evidence can still be found that can police make arrests. Even a laboratory that has been scrubbed clean may yield evidence of drug production. Drugs or other incriminating substances may be found inside the plumbing by using instruments called borescopes and fiberscopes. These are cameras attached to tubes so they can "see" around corners and inside the plumbing. Once located, these residual substances can be recovered and analyzed. Drug producers may think they can avoid arrest by simply loading up their equipment and moving to a new location. The trace evidence they leave behind inside their pipes, though, may be enough to get them busted.[15]

policies issued in the names of addicts, is perhaps the most heinous and perverted form of financial fraud in the United States to date.[16]

TYPE 2 DRUG CRIMES

Secondary, or type 2, drug crimes are crimes committed by addicts in order to pay for their drug habit. It usually does not take state-of-the-art equipment, or massive operations involving teams of law enforcement agencies, to solve these crimes. Usually it takes no more than a crime scene investigator (CSI), a fingerprint expert, and one smart cop. The CSI finds the prints, and a latent print examiner evaluates and compares the prints. These crimes, because they are committed by addicts, are usually not very sophisticated. Common drug-related crimes are car theft and carjacking. Cars are stolen to sell, or for one-time use in crimes, and to transport drugs from city to city. One innovative thief would steal a car, then "rent" it to drug dealers. Another, in order to steal the car, would gently rear-end the car he wanted then carjack it when the owner got out to inspect the vehicle's damage. Some big-city police department crime labs process about one carjacked car a day.

Even though muggings, burglaries, and robberies are often solved, as long as there are addicts there will also be type 2 crimes. The best way to lessen the number of secondary drug crimes is to decrease the number of addicts.[17]

FIGHTING FOR DRUG-DEALING TURF

Other drug-related crimes are acts of violence, such as assault and murder, committed by a drug-dealing organization in order to expand its "turf," or area of operation. Drug-related shootings and murders are common in many large American cities. And it does not stop with just one shooting. A shooting often leads to retaliation, which then leads to more retaliation. And drug gangs are not appreciative of witnesses who do their civic duty, often shooting them down or burning them out. During the summer of 2006 such a series of crimes was busted in Peoria, Illinois.

A former Chicago Hells Angels leader, Melvin Chancey, 38, and two others were behind shootings, beatings, and threats against rival gang members and others to clear the way for drug deals in northern Illinois. The conspiracy protected sales of cocaine and methamphetamine with a street value of $624,000 from 1993 through 2002, according to prosecutors. Chancey pleaded guilty in January 2006 to federal racketeering and drug charges, admitting that he dealt cocaine and methamphetamine in the 1990s while conspiring with fellow bikers to threaten and intimidate other motorcycle gangs. Chancey admitted that he took part in the 1994 shooting of a rival club member, along with a 1995 scheme where threats were made to blow up a rival gang's clubhouse in Kanka-kee. His plea deal shaved about 10 years off his potential sentence. Chancey was sentenced to nine years in prison for his part in a decade-long racketeering and narcotics ring. Other former Hells Angels chapter leaders caught in the federal investigation included two who were sentenced to three- and four-year prison sentences, respectively, a month earlier in the scheme.[18]

MURDER BY DRUGS

Law enforcement officials are always looking for new and better ways to prosecute drug dealers. During the summer of 2006 there was a cluster of drug-overdose deaths in the Midwest. Examinations by the medical examiner showed that the victims were heroin addicts who had overdosed because they had injected themselves with a deadly concoction.[19] The heroin had been mixed with a second painkiller, a drug called fentanyl, which has been estimated to be 50 times more powerful than morphine.[20]

The combination, for many of its users, had turned out to be deadly. When police in Chicago, Illinois, arrested a drug dealer, 35-year-old Corey Crump, who had been selling the heroin/fentanyl combination, they didn't just charge him with drug dealing, they charged him with murder.[21]

Crump had a history of drug arrests. Now he was being charged with the death of 17-year-old Joseph Krecker, who had been found slumped over in his car not long after buying heroin from Crump in a Chicago suburb. The victim had only driven a couple of blocks when he died at the wheel. The teenaged victim happened to be the son of Deputy Chief Jack Krecker of the suburban Franklin Park police.[22]

According to the *New York Times*, by the summer of 2006, heroin mixed with fentanyl had been responsible for the overdose deaths of almost 200 people, with about three-quarters of them dying in Cook County, which is Chicago and its surrounding area.[23]

"This is growing like wild," said the Cook County medical examiner, Edmund Donoghue. Police officials told the press that gangs and drug dealers have been "so spooked" by the investigations by local and federal police that they are often forcing buyers to use the drug inside the apartments where it is sold, in front of them, to avoid detection.[24]

The death-by-fentanyl phenomenon reached New York City that same summer. The New York Police Department announced that there had been 23 deaths from heroin cut with fentanyl by mid-September 2006.[25]

Although 2006 is the last year for which complete figures are available, the spike in heroin fatalities had not abated by the spring of 2008.[26]

IS THE WAR BEING WON?

For all of the money that has been spent on the War on Drugs since 1988, is law enforcement winning? According to Richard Gray, an assistant professor of criminal justice at Fairleigh Dickinson University and a retired drug abuse treatment coordinator for the U.S. Probation Department in Brooklyn, New York, about the best that can be said is that the authorities are holding their own.[27] According to the annual National Household Survey on Drug Abuse conducted by the U.S. Department of Health and Human Services, drug abuse by persons older than 12 has remained about the same since the Office of National Drug Control Policy (ONDCP) was formed in 1988. The office was established by the Anti-Drug Abuse Act. According the White House Drug Policy Web site, "the ONDCP's purpose is to establish policies, priorities, and objectives for the Nation's drug control program. The goals of the program are to reduce illicit drug use, manufacturing, and trafficking, drug-related crime and violence, and drug-related health consequences."[28] Although crime is down significantly across the board since 1988, drug-related arrests have remained about the same. There are still about 1.5 million drug-related arrests each

⚲ THE "DRUG CZAR": HEAD OF THE ONDCP

The top general in the battle against drugs in the United States is the director of the ONDCP, more commonly known as the drug czar. Since December 7, 2001, that man has been John P. Walters. The drug czar decides how his agency spends its money and sets priorities. When he took the job Walters said his goal was to use education to decrease drug use in teenagers by 10 percent. The ONDCP's Monitoring the Future study done two years later showed that drug use by American teens was down 11 percent, better than the czar's goal. Another one of Walters' programs is Plan Colombia. In 2003 hundreds of thousands of acres of coca fields in Colombia were poisoned and killed. That prevented about 500 tons of cocaine from entering the United States. It also cost the drug barons in Colombia hundreds of millions of dollars in profits.[29]

year in the United States, about the same as when the War on Drugs began.[30]

Importantly, the 2005 National Household Survey on Drug Abuse (NHSDA) found that high school students find drugs as easy to get as their counterparts did 20 years earlier. That study also found that marijuana was judged to be easy or very easy to get by 85 percent of high school seniors, and 40 percent thought LSD and cocaine were easily accessible.[31]

Professor Gray believes it is time to re-prioritize the War on Drugs. He wrote: "Has the drug war decreased drug-related crime? Is the availability of illegal substances down? Insofar as the 'War on Drugs' metaphor has failed us, we had best begin to think of a new strategy."

EDUCATION

One of the most modern methods to combat drugs is education. The public must be educated as to the dangers of drugs, and law enforcement needs to stay educated as to the latest way to fight drugs. In

2008 the Office of National Drug Control Policy operated several anti-drug programs. These programs included:

- A media campaign, which included resources for parents, and outlined how parents could monitor their teens' possible drug use, public service announcements for television and radio, a Marijuana Awareness Kit, and more instructions for parents on how to determine if their child is getting high.
- Drug-Free Communities and Drug-Free Workplace programs designed to reduce drug use among youth and adults by addressing the factors in a community and in the workplace that increase the risk of substance abuse.
- High-Intensity Drug Trafficking Areas program, which identifies such areas so crime prevention assets can be focused upon the correct locales.
- Counterdrug Technology Assessment Center, which sees to it that the government's anti-drug forces are always using state-of-the-art technology in their investigations.
- Access to Recovery. According to the ONDCP, as many as 100,000 Americans every year seek medical treatment for their drug problems but are not treated because they cannot find an appropriate treatment center, or can't afford one if they do. In his 2006 State of the Union address, President George W. Bush announced a three-year, $600 million federal program to help

♀ DARE

The organization known as Drug Abuse Resistance Education (DARE) was founded in 1983 in Los Angeles, with the objective of giving school children the necessary skills to avoid involvement in drugs, gangs, and violence. The program in L.A. was so successful that, by 2008, it had spread to three-quarters of the school districts in the United States, and to 43 countries. Through the program, classrooms are visited by police officers who are street smart and have been trained in how to answer the questions most often asked by students about drugs and crime.[32]

⚲ TOUR OF THE DEA MUSEUM

According to their Web site, the DEA Museum and Visitors Center's mission is to "educate the American public on the history of drugs, drug addiction and drug law enforcement in the United States through engaging and state-of-the-art exhibits, displays, interactive stations, and educational outreach programs."[33]

The museum, located in Arlington, Virginia, not far from Washington, D.C., opened in 1989. The museum, which is across the street from the Pentagon City Mall, is open from 10:00 a.m. to 4:00 p.m., Tuesday to Friday. Admission is free. The museum welcomes group tours but recommends calling ahead for reservations for groups of 15 or more persons. Of course, there is a gift shop.[34]

The museum also does its part to educate those who cannot visit about the battle to prevent drug smuggling and drug sales, and about the dangers of drug abuse. The museum's traveling exhibit, "Target America: Opening Eyes to the Damage Drugs Cause," tours the country. The schedule is posted online at http://www.targetamerica.org/exhibitdates.html.[35]

those Americans who are suffering from drug abuse and addiction to get free medical treatment.

- Student Drug Testing program examines the legal issues and public health goals associated with possible future testing of students for drugs. Such a testing program, were it to become a reality, would deter children from drug use, and identify children who need help.[36]

Chronology

1729 Opium smoking is made illegal in China. The poppy had been known in China since at least A.D. 700, but it was only in the 1600s that the Chinese realized opium mixed with tobacco could be smoked to get high. This innovation ultimately led to a mounting number of junkies and a new law passed making the smoking of opium illegal.

1803 Morphine, a highly addictive painkiller, is first processed from raw opium by Frederick Sertürner, and named after Morpheus, the Greek God of Dreams.

1853 The hypodermic needle, which would be used to inject drugs directly into the human bloodstream, is invented. At the time it was called the "hollow needle."

1874 Heroin is invented, processed in a lab in St. Mary's Hospital in London from morphine.

1898 The Bayer Company, famous for its aspirin, markets heroin as a legal painkiller. At the time it was believed that the painkiller was less addictive than morphine.

1914 Before many drugs were illegal in North America, the United States attempted to tax drug dealers through the Harrison Narcotics Act, passed in 1914. Dealers who did not pay the appropriate tax were subject to arrest by agents of the Bureau of Internal Revenue, the predecessor of today's Internal Revenue Service (IRS).

1920 The Dangerous Drug Act prohibits the possession and use of heroin "without a medical purpose." Heroin would no longer be available over-the-counter.

1922 U.S. Congress passes the Narcotic Import and Export Act, making it illegal to import opium, except for medical use.

1923 Formation of Interpol, which has become the world's largest police organization.

1924 *June* U.S. Congress passes the Heroin Act, making it illegal to manufacture or possess heroin. By the time this law was enacted it was estimated that 98 percent of all New York City junkies were hooked on heroin.

1930 The Federal Bureau of Narcotics is formed as an agency of the U.S. Department of the Treasury. It was during the first years of this organization's existence that many of the drugs that are still the scourge of society today were first made illegal.

1937 Marijuana is declared illegal in the United States.

1938 LSD is invented by chemist Albert Hofmann in Sandoz Laboratories in Basel, Switzerland. He invented the drug and, using himself as a human guinea pig, was the first to experience its effects.

1966 The Bureau of Drug Abuse Control (BDAC) is created as part of the Food and Drug Administration.

1967 *June* Release of the Beatles' album *Sgt. Pepper's Lonely Hearts Club Band* helps to popularize marijuana and LSD with lyrics such as "Lucy in the sky with diamonds" and "I'd love to turn you on."

LSD is declared illegal in the United States.

1968 The BDAC and the Federal Bureau of Narcotics (FBN) join together and the Bureau of Narcotics and Dangerous Drugs (BNDD) is born.

1970 The Controlled Substances Act is passed, dividing drugs into categories and setting penalties for possessing and selling different types of drugs.

1973 Birth of the Drug Enforcement Administration (DEA), a division of the Department of Justice. It has 1,470 special agents and an annual budget of $75 million.

1988 Office of National Drug Control Policy (ONDCP) created to centrally coordinate legislative, security, diplomatic, research, and health policy throughout the government. This program, started under the Reagan Administration, is considered the start of the modern War on Drugs.

1992   The National Criminal Intelligence Service (NCIS) is formed. This is the British national police force in charge of fighting drugs in Great Britain.

1993   The North American Free Trade Agreement (NAFTA) goes into effect, increasing trade across the Mexican border, thus complicating the jobs of U.S. Customs officials trying to stop drug smuggling.

2000   U.S. President Bill Clinton gives $1.3 billion in aid to Colombia to decrease cocaine production and spray coca fields with herbicide.

2003   *April* The Illicit Drug Anti-Proliferation Act is enacted, targeting the illegal production and sale of chemical drugs such as Ecstasy and methamphetamine.

2004   The U.S. Department of State, of Defense, and the DEA work together to implement the Counternarcotics Implementation Plan, reducing heroin production in Afghanistan.

2006   Police discover a half-mile long tunnel connecting a warehouse in Tijuana with a warehouse in the U.S. More than two tons of marijuana is seized.

Endnotes

Introduction

1. Interpol, "Drugs and criminal organizations," Interpol Online. http://www.interpol.int/Public/Drugs/default.asp. Downloaded October 2, 2006.
2. Ibid.
3. FoxNews.com, "Venezuela Leader Accuses DEA of Espionage," Fox News. http://www.foxnews.com/story/0,2933,165011,00.html. Posted August 19, 2005.
4. FoxNews.com, "DEA Busts 160 in Drug Transportation Rings," Fox News. http://www.foxnews.com/story/0,2933,166262 ,00.html. Posted August 19, 2005.

Chapter 1

1. United States Department of Justice, "DEA Busts International Cocaine Trafficking Ring," United States Department of Justice. http://www.usdoj.gov/dea/pubs/pressrel/pr113005.html. Posted November 30, 2005.
2. Ibid.
3. United States Coast Guard, "U.S. Coast Guard Drug Interdiction, Coast Guard Office of Law Enforcement." http://www.uscg.mil/hq/cg5/cg531/drug_interdiction.asp. Accessed October 8, 2008.

4. Michael Benson, *The U.S. Coast Guard* (Minneapolis, Minn.: Lerner Publications Company, 2005), 36–37.
5. Jillean Powell, *Crimebusters: Drug Trafficking* (Brookfield, Conn.: Copper Beech Books, 1997), 5.
6. Ibid.
7. Rich Sleeman, Jim Carter, and Karl Ebejer, "Drugs on Money and Beyond: tandem mass spectrometry in the forensic sciences," *Spectroscopy Europe*. http://www.spectroscopyeurope.com/MS1_17_6.pdf. Downloaded October 10, 2006.
8. Rensselaer Polytechnic Institute, "Chromatography," Rensselaer Polytechnic Institute. http://www.rpi.edu/dept/chem-eng/Biotech-Environ/CHROMO/chromintro.html. Downloaded October 1, 2006.
9. American Society for Mass Spectrometry, "Why should you be interested in Mass Spectrometry?," American Society for Mass Spectrometry. http://www.asms.org/whatisms/p1.html. Downloaded October 1, 2006.

Chapter 2

1. Cowley College Alumni Newsletter, "From daring rescue to major drug bust:

Former Cowley student has seen it all with U.S. Coast Guard," Cowley College Alumni Newsletter Online. http://www.cowley.edu/news/alumni/newsletter. Downloaded September 27, 2006.

2. Benson, 37.
3. Cowley College Alumni Newsletter.
4. Ibid.
5. Ibid.
6. Michael Benson, D. O. Coulson, and A. Swenson, *The Complete Idiot's Guide to National Security* (New York: Alpha Books, 2003), 121–122.
7. United States Navy, "The War on Drugs continues on Land and at Sea," United States Navy Online. http://www.navy.com/about/navylife/onduty/navyglobalinvolvement/preventing/. Downloaded September 26, 2006.
8. Michael Isikoff, "A Deal with the Devil," *Newsweek*, October 30, 1995.
9. "Operation Just Cause," Global Security: Reliable Security Information. http://www.globalsecurity.org/military/ops/just_cause.htm. Downloaded September 3, 2006.

Chapter 3
1. C.A. Sullivan, "Customs Air Power: Staying on Top of Change," *Air Beat* 22, 4 (July/August 1993): 4–6, 22–23. http://www.ncjrs.gov/App/Publications/abstract.a

spx?ID=144564. Accessed May 16, 2008.
2. Ibid.
3. Ibid.
4. "Mexicans seize huge cocaine haul." http://www.news.bbc.co.uk/2/hi/Americas/4901828.stm. Posted April 12, 2006. Accessed May 2, 2008.
5. Lauren Monsen, "South America Makes Progress on Drugs, Despite Ongoing Challenges," U.S. State Department Web site. http://America.gov. Posted March 2, 2006. Accessed May 2, 2008.
6. Benson, *Coast Guard*, 43.
7. Louis A. Arana-Barradas, "Airmen, drug runners play game of cat and mouse." http://www.af.mil. Posted August 6, 2007. Accessed May 2, 2008.
8. Benson, *Coast Guard*, 4.
9. Powell, 11.

Chapter 4
1. Voice of America, "Japan Makes One of World's Biggest Drug Busts," Voice of America News. http://www.help-for-you.com/news/Oct2001/Oct27/PRT27-59Article.html. Posted October 27, 2001.
2. Carmen Sesin, "Caring for 'drug mules' who perish on the job," MSNBC. http://www.msnbc.msn.com/id/5050399/. Posted May 25, 2004.
3. John P. Gilbride, Special Agent-in-Charge, New York Division, U.S. Drug Enforcement Administration,

press release dated February 1, 2006.

4. Sesin, op. cit.
5. Ibid.
6. Ibid.
7. Ibid.
8. Ibid.
9. Jerome Socolovsky, "Europe Deals with Growing Cocaine Trade," National Public Radio. http://www.npr.org. Posted October 24, 2007. Accessed May 5, 2008.
10. WCBS-TV newscast, September 12, 2006.

Chapter 5

1. J.L. O'Neill, "Asset Forfeiture," A paper presented at the Second Annual Symposium on Criminal Justice Issues, August 23–26, 1987, Chicago, Ill. http://www.ncjrs.gov/App/publications/abstract.aspx?ID=117652. Accessed May 16, 2008.
2. Heather Gunas, "Supreme Court Review of Drug Forfeiture Cases." http://www.druglibrary.org/schaffer/misc/ct/drugforf2.html. Accessed May 16, 2008.
3. Sam Crawford, "Undercover Game Plan to Crack Missouri's Blue Capsule Conspiracy," *Official Detective Stories* (June 1977): 46–51.
4. "DEA Busts Georgia's First Meth 'Super-Lab'," United States Department of Justice. http://www.usdoj.gov/dea/pu bs/states/newsrel/

atlanta021405.html. Posted February 14, 2005.
5. Ibid.
6. Ibid.
7. Ibid.
8. Ibid.
9. Fox News.com, "DEA Busts 160 in Drug Transportation Rings," Fox News. http://www.foxnews.com/story/0,2933,166262,00.html. Posted August 19, 2005.
10. Ibid.

Chapter 6

1. Christopher Goffard, "Accuracy of drug dogs is challenged," *St. Petersburg Times*, August 19, 2003, A7.
2. Maria D. Martirano, "Call about suspicious person leads to drug arrest at Bel Air," *Cumberland Times-News*, October 3, 2001.
3. Southern Hills Kennels: Bomb and Drug Detection Dogs. http://www.drugdogs.net.
4. Goffard, op. cit.
5. Linda Shrieves, "A nose for trouble—and teamwork," *Orlando Sentinel*, April 13, 2002.
6. Goffard, op. cit.

Chapter 7

1. Steve Butcher and Andrea Petrie, "Police Net Record Ecstasy Haul," *The Age* Online. http://www.theage.com.au/news/National/Police-net-record-ecstasy-haul/2005/04/15/1113509926817.html. Posted

April 16, 2005. Accessed
May 8, 2008.

2. Author interview with private
investigator Vincent Parco,
October 3, 2006.

Chapter 8

1. C.J. Schexnayder, "Watchdog
Challenges U.S. Drug War in
Colombia," *San Francisco
Chronicle*, December 7, 2005.
http://www.commondreams.
org/headlines05/1207-07.htm.
Accessed May 12, 2008.

2. Ibid.

3. Powell, 11.

4. Fox News, "Venezuela
Leader Accuses DEA of
Espionage," Fox News.com.
http://www.foxnews.com/
story/0,2933,165011,00.html.
com. Posted August 7, 2005.

5. John Otis, "Colombia's War
on Drugs Getting Hotter:
U.S. Pumps in $862 million;
Skeptics Wonder if it Will
Help," *Houston Chronicle*.
http://www.chron.com/
disp/story.mpl/special/
drugquagmire/603933.html.
Posted July 15, 2000.

6. Ibid.

7. Ibid.

8. Michael Howie, "Warning
as £1bn drug-smuggling ring
is smashed," *The Scotsman*.
http://news.scotsman.com/
drugspolicy/Warning-as-61m
-drugsmuggling-ring.2764845.
jp.man.com. Posted January 7,
2006.

9. Paula Dear and Chris Summers, "Bringing down the

Colombian connection," BBC
News. http://www.News.bbc.
co.uk/2/hi/uk_news/4534255.
stm. Posted January 6, 2006.
Accessed May 12, 2008.

10. Ibid.

11. Ibid.

12. Ibid.

13. "Local Gang Bust Earns
National Recognition."
Department of Justice News
Release, available at http://
www.psn.gov/press/07sep18.
html. Posted September
18, 2007. Accessed June
10, 2008; and biography of
Professor G. Robert Blakey
on the University of Notre
Dame Web site, available at
http://law.nd.edu/people/
faculty-and-administration/
teaching-and-research-faculty/
g-robert-blakey. Accessed June
10, 2008.

14. Dear and Summers.

Chapter 9

1. Lynda Hurst, "Turkey did it.
Can Afghanistan?" *The Star*.
http://www.thestar.com/
comment/columnists/article/
185452. Posted February 25,
2007. Accessed May 12,
2008.

2. "Eyewitness: Golden Triangle Opium Fields." http://
news.bbc.co.uk/2/hi/asia-
pacific/1768035.stm. Posted
January 18, 2002. Accessed
June 10, 2008.

3. Iran Focus, "Iran tops world
drug addiction rate list—
report." http://www.iranfocus.

com/en/index.php?option=
com_content&task=view&id
=3805. Posted September 24,
2005. Accessed May 12, 2008.

4. Ibid.

5. Hoobler, 45.

6. Hoobler, 48.

7. Anne W. Patterson, "Release of
the 2007 International Narcotics Control Strategy Report."
http://www.state.gov/p/inl/rls/
rm/81278.htm.

8. Hoobler, 46.

9. "Statement of Steven W.
Casteel, Assistant Administrator for Intelligence Before
to Senate Committee on the
Judiciary, May 20, 2003."
http://www.justice.gov/dea/
pubs/cngrtest/ct052003.html.

10. Ibid.

Chapter 10

1. Drug Enforcement
Administration, "A Tradition
of Excellence," U.S. Drug
Enforcement Administration.
http://www.usdoj.gov/dea/
pubs/history/1970-1975.html.
Downloaded May 22, 2006.

2. WKION-46 Television Station,
"DEA busts manufacturer
suspected of lacing candy and
soda with marijuana," WKION
Online. http://www.kion46.
com. Posted March 17, 2006.

3. Don Thompson, "Cartels
Use Suburban Homes to
Grow Pot," America Online/
Associated Press. http://
impossible.newsvine.com/_
news/2006/09/27/376851-cartels-
use-suburban-homes-to-grow-
pot. Posted September 27,
2006.

4. Ibid.

5. Jaquelyn Nixon, "DEA busts
Ecstasy lab on campus,"
Michigan Daily. http://media.
www.michigandaily.com/
media/storage/paper851/
news/2001/10/17/News/
Dea-Busts.Ecstasy.Lab.
On.Campus-1406944.shtml.
Posted October 17, 2001.

6. Ibid.

7. Ibid.

8. Ibid.

9. Ibid.

10. Ibid.

11. Ibid.

12. Europol, "Successful operations against major drugs
network," Europol Online.
http://www.europol.europa.eu/
index.asp?page=news&news=p
r060201.htm. Posted February
1, 2006.

13. Bob Sullivan, "Drug ring
indicted in odd identity
theft case: Authorities say
life insurance polices taken
out on addicts," MSNBC.
http://www.msnbc.msn.com/
id/5166112. Posted June 8,
2004.

14. Ibid.

15. Global Borescope. http://www.
fiberscope.net/borescope_
fiberscope_fiber_optic_scope.
html#flex.

16. Sullivan, op. cit..

17. National Institute on Drug
Abuse, "Principles of Drug
Addiction Treatment,"

National Institute on Drug Abuse. http://www.nida. nih.gov/podat/PODATIndex. html. Posted February 8, 2005. Accessed October 9, 2006.

18. Newday, "Ex-Hells Angels Leader Gets Nine Years," Fox News. http://origin.foxnews. com/wires/2006Jul26/0,4670, HellsAngelsSentence,00.html. Posted July 26,2006.

19. Eric Ferkenhoff, "Murder Charges Filed in Death From Painkiller-Laced Heroin," *New York Times*. http://www. nytimes.com/2006/08/25/ us/25chicago.html?_r=1&scp=1 &sq=Murder%20Charges%20F iled%20in%20Death%20&st=c se&oref=slogin. Posted August 25, 2006.

20. 1010 WINS, "NYPD: Over-doses in Queens Point to Tainted Heroin," 1010 WINS Radio. http://www.1010wins. com. Posted September 13, 2006.

21. Ferkenhoff, op.cit.

22. Ibid.

23. Ibid.

24. Ibid.

25. "NYPD: Overdoses . . .," op. cit.

26. "Drug deaths soar in Boston," Official Web site of the *Boston Globe*. http://www.boston. com. Posted in May 2008. Accessed May 13, 2008.

27. Richard Gray, "War on Drugs," *FCU Magazine* (Summer/Fall 2006): 20.

28. Substance Abuse and Mental Health Services Administra-tion. http://www.samhsa.gov/ About/background.aspx.

29. United Nations Office of Drug and Crime, "Colombia." http://unodc.org/pdf/ publications/colombia_report_ 2003-09-25.pdf. Accessed May 13, 2008.

30. Gray, op. cit.

31. Ibid.

32. "About D.A.R.E. The Official D.A.R.E. Web Site." http:// www.dare.com/home/about– dare.asp. Accessed May 13, 2008.

33. DEA Museum. http://www. deamuseum.org/museum_ aboutus.html.

34. Ibid.

35. United Nations Office of Drug and Crime, "Colombia."

36. Ibid.

Glossary

addict A person who is hooked on a drug and must keep taking the drug to avoid feeling bad.

baron Leader of a drug-trafficking organization.

cartel Organization designed to traffic drugs.

chromatography A popular testing method to determine if a substance is, or contains, illegal drugs.

cut Diluting drugs by adding look-alike materials, for example lactose and milk sugar added to cocaine or heroin, creating the illusion that the consumer is getting more than he or she actually is.

hallucinogens Drugs, such as LSD, mescaline, and mushrooms, that alter sensory perceptions.

informant Someone inside a criminal organization, or with knowledge of that organization, who tells police what they know.

junkie One addicted to a drug.

jurisdiction Region of land or water in which a particular law enforcement agency has power.

M.O. Method of operation or, in Latin, *Modus Operandi*; the way in which a criminal commits his or her crimes.

money laundering Investing or spending money earned from committing a crime so that the criminal no longer has in his possession cash that might connect him to the crime.

reagent Substance used to identify drugs; a reagent turns a vivid color when mixed with drugs.

surveillance Police term for spying.

trafficking The production, transportation, and sale of illegal drugs.

wiretap Listening devices that allow authorities to listen in on other people's phone conversations.

withdrawal Painful experience and physical reaction when a person quits addictive drugs.

Bibliography

Books and Magazines

Benson, Michael. *The U.S. Coast Guard*. Minneapolis, Minn.: Lerner Publications Company, 2005.

Benson, M., D.O. Coulson, and A. Swenson. *The Complete Idiot's Guide to National Security*. New York: Alpha Books, 2003..

Castillo, E. Eduardo. "Mexico Army Finds Tons of Cocaine on Plane," *Newsday*. April 12, 2006.

Crawford, Sam. "Undercover Game Plan to Crack Missouri's Blue Capsule Conspiracy," *Official Detective Stories* (June 1977): 46–51.

Dandurat, Karen. "The Methamphetamine Menace," *Portsmouth Herald*. October 8, 2006.

Goffard, Christopher. "Accuracy of Drug Dogs is Challenged," *St. Petersburg Times*. August 19, 2003, A7.

Gray, Richard. "War on Drugs," *FDU Magazine* 14, 1 (Summer/Fall 2006): 20.

Gunn, J.W., Jr. "The Bureau of Drug Abuse Control," *Journal of Forensic Science* 13, 3 (July 1968): 302–317.

Harris, Neil. *Understanding Drugs: Drugs and Crime*. London, England: Aladdin Books, 1989.

Knopf, Richard L. *Illusion or Victory: How the U.S. Navy SEALS Win America's Failing War on Drugs*. New York: S.P.I. Books, 1997.

Web Sites

Associated Press. "Former Hells Angels leader sentenced in racketeering scheme." Available online. URL: http://groups. google.co.uk/group/alt.true-crime/browse_thread/thread/ 0b5f14bff7856cce/794b665a582d7c21?hl=en. Posted July 26, 2006.

"Before Prohibition," Addiction Research Unit of the Department of Psychology at the University of Buffalo. Available online. URL: http://wings.buffalo.edu/aru/pre prohibition.htm. Downloaded October 10, 2006.

Butcher, Steve, and Andrea Petrie. "Police Net Record Ecstasy Haul," *The Age* Online. Available online. URL: http://www.theage.com. au/news/National/Police-net-record-ecstasy-haul/2005/04/15/1113 509926817.html. Posted April 16, 2005

"Can We Win the War on Drugs This Way?" DRCNet Online Library of Drug Policy. Available online. URL: http://www.druglibrary. org/schaffer/library/basicfax7.htm. Downloaded October 10, 2006.

Castillo, E. Eduardo. "Mexico Army Finds Tons of Cocaine on Plane," *Newsday,* April 12, 2006. Available online at http://www. dominicantoday.com/dr/world/2006/4/12/12365/print. Accessed June 10, 2008.

"Chromatography," Rensselaer Polytechnic Institute. Available online. URL: http://www.rpi.edu/dept/chem-eng/Biotech-Environ/ CHROMO/chromintro.html. Downloaded October 1. 2006.

"DEA Busts Georgia's First Meth 'Super-Lab'," U.S. Department of Justice. Available online. URL: http://www.usdoj.gov/dea/pubs/ states/newsrel/atlanta021405.html. Posted February 14, 2005.

"DEA Busts Manufacturer Suspected of Lacing Candy and Soda with Marijuana," KION-46 TV. URL: http://www.kion46.com. Posted March 17, 2006. No longer accessible.

"DEA Busts 160 in Drug Transportation Rings," Fox News. Available online. URL: http://www.foxnews.com/story/0,2933,166262,00. html. Posted August 19, 2005.

Drug Enforcement Administration Museum Visitors Center on the Web. Available online. URL: http://www.deamuseum.org.

"Drugs and criminal organizations," Interpol on the Web. Available online. URL: http://www.interpol.int/Public/Drugs/default.asp. Downloaded October 2, 2006.

Ferkenhoff, Eric. "Murder Charges Filed in Death From Painkiller-Laced Heroin," *New York Times.* Available online. URL: http:// www.nytimes.com/2006/08/25/us/25chicago.html. Posted August 25, 2006.

"From daring rescue to major drug bust: Former Cowley student has seen it all with U.S. Coast Guard," Cowley College Alumni Newsletter. Available online. URL: http://www.cowley.edu/news/ alumni/newsletter. Posted in October 2004.

"History of Heroin," United Nations Office on Drugs and Crime. Available online. URL: http://www.unodc.org/unodc/en/data-and-analysis/bulletin/bulletin_1953-01-01_2_page004.html. Downloaded October 1, 2006.

Howie, Michael. "Warning as £1bn drug-smuggling ring is smashed," *The Scotsman* on the Web. Available online. URL: http://news. scotsman.com/drugspolicy/Warning-as-61m-drugsmuggling-ring.2764845.jp. Posted January 7, 2006.

"Inventors: Hypodermic Needle," About.com. Available online. URL: http://inventors.about.com/library/inventors/blsyringe.htm. Downloaded October 10, 2006.

"Japan Makes One of World's Biggest Drug Busts," Voice of America News. Available online. URL: http://www.help-for-you.com/news/ Oct2001/Oct27/PRT27-59Article.html. Posted October 27, 2001.

"John P. Walters, Office of National Drug Control Policy, Director," Office of National Drug Control Policy. Available online. URL: http://www.whitehouse.gov/government/walters-bio.html. Downloaded October 1, 2006.

LaMotte, Ellen N. "History of the Opium Trade in China," DRCNet Online Library of Drug Policy. Available online. URL: http:// www.druglibrary.org/schaffer/history/om/om15.htm. Downloaded October 10, 2006.

Martirano, Maria D. "Call About Suspicious Person Leads to Drug Arrest at Bel Air," *Columbia Times-News*. Available online. URL: http://www.times-news.com. Posted October 3, 2001.

"Morphine's 200th birthday, May 21," *Medical News Today*. Available online. URL: http://www.medicalnewstoday.c om/articles/24715. php. Posted May 19, 2005.

"The Narcotic Detector Dog," Southern Star Ranch K9 Training Center. Available online. URL: http://www.narcoticdogs.com. Downloaded June 1, 2006.

Nixon, Jacquelyn. "DEA busts Ecstasy lab on campus," *Michigan Daily*. Available online. URL: http://media.www.michigandaily. com/media/storage/paper851/news/2001/10/17/News/Dea-Busts. Ecstasy.Lab.On.Campus-14 06944.shtml. Posted October 17, 2001.

"NYPD: Overdoses in Queens Point to Tainted Heroin," 1010 Wins Radio. Available online. URL: http://www.1010wins.com. Posted on September 13, 2006.

Office of National Drug Control Policy. Available online. URL: http:// www.whitehousedrugpolicy.gov.

Otis, John. "Colombia's war on drugs getting hotter: U.S. Pumps in $862 Million; Skeptics Wonder if it Will Help," *Houston Chronicle*. Available online. URL: http://www.chron.com/disp/ story.mpl/special/drugquagmire/603933.html. Posted July 15, 2000.

"Principles of Drug Addiction Treatment," National Institute on Drug Abuse. Available online. URL: http://www.nida.nih.gov/podat/ PODATIndex.html. Posted February 8, 2005.

Sesin, Carmen. "Caring for 'Drug Mules' Who Perish on the Job," MSNBC. Available online. URL: http://www.msnbc.msn.com/ id/5050399. Posted May 25, 2004.

Shrieves, Linda. "A Nose for Trouble—and Teamwork," *Orlando Sentinel*. Available online. URL: http://www.orlandosentinel.com. Posted April 13, 2002.

Sleeman, R., J. Carter, and K. Ebejer. "Drugs on Money and Beyond: Tandem Mass Spectrometry in the Forensic Sciences," *Spectroscopy Europe*. Available online. URL: http://www.spectroscopyeurope.com/MS1_17_6.pdf. Downloaded October 10, 2006.

Southern Hills Kennels in New Smyrna Beach, Florida. Available online. URL: http://www.drugdogs.net. Accessed May 15, 2008.

Substance Abuse and Mental Health Services Administration. Available online. URL: http://www.samhsa.gov. Accessed May 15, 2008.

"Successful Operations Against Major Drugs Network," Europol. Available online. URL: http://www.europol.europa.eu/index.asp?page=news&news=pr060201.htm. Posted February 1, 2006.

Sullivan, Bob. "Drug Ring Indicted in Odd Identity Theft Case: Authorities Say Life Insurance Polices Taken Out on Addicts," MSNBC. Available online. URL: http://www.msnbc.msn.com/id/5166112. Posted June 8, 2004.

"The War on Drugs Continues on Land and at Sea," U.S. Navy. Available online. URL: http://www.navy.com/about/navylife/onduty/navyglobalinvolvement/preventing/. Downloaded September 26, 2006.

Thompson, Don. "Cartels Use Suburban Homes to Grow Pot," America Online/Associated Press. Available online. URL: http://impossible.newsvine.com/_news/2006/09/27/376851-cartels-use-suburban-homes-to-grow-pot. Posted September 26, 2006.

"A Tradition of Excellence," Drug Enforcement Adminstration. Available online. URL: http://www.us doj.gov/dea/pubs/history/1970-1975.html. Downloaded May 22, 2006.

"U.S. Coast Guard Drug Interdiction, Coast Guard Office of Law Enforcement," United States Coast Guard. Available online. http://www.uscg.mil/hq/cg5/cg531/drug_interdiction.asp. Accessed October 8, 2008.

"Venezuela Leader Accuses DEA of Espionage," Fox News. Available online. URL: http://www.foxnews.com/story/0,2933,165011,00.html. Posted August 7, 2005.

"Why should you be interested in mass Spectrometry?," The American Society for Mass Spectrometry. Available online. URL: http://www.asms.org/whatisms/p1.html. Downloaded October 1, 2006.

Further Resources

Books

Benson, Michael. *The U.S. Coast Guard*. Minneapolis, Minn.: Lerner Publications Company, 2005.

Gaines, Larry K., and Peter B. Kraska, eds. *Drugs, Crime and Justice*. Long Grove, Ill.: Waveland Press, 2002.

Powell, Jillian. *Crimebusters: Drug Trafficking*. Brookfield, Conn.: Copper Beech Books, 1997.

Walker, Samuel. *Sense and Nonsense: About Crime and Drugs*. Florence, Ky.: Wadsworth Publishing, 2005.

Web Sites

Drug Enforcement Administration
http://www.usdoj.gov/dea/index.htm

KidsHealth
http://www.kidshealth.org

National Institute on Drug Abuse
http://www.drugabuse.gov/

Index

About the Author

Michael Benson is the author or co-author of 41 books, including the true-crime books *Betrayal in Blood* and *Lethal Embrace*. He's also written *The Encyclopedia of the JFK Assassination* and *Complete Idiot's Guides to NASA, National Security, The CIA, Submarines,* and *Modern China*. Other works include biographies of Ronald Reagan, Bill Clinton, and William Howard Taft. Originally from Rochester, N.Y., he is a graduate of Hofstra University.

About the Consulting Editor

John L. French is a 31-year veteran of the Baltimore City Police Crime Laboratory. He is currently a crime laboratory supervisor. His responsibilities include responding to crime scenes, overseeing the preservation and collection of evidence, and training crime scene technicians. He has been actively involved in writing the operating procedures and technical manual for his unit and has conducted training in numerous areas of crime scene investigation. In addition to his crime scene work, Mr. French is also a published author, specializing in crime fiction. His short stories have appeared in *Alfred Hitchcock's Mystery Magazine* and numerous anthologies.